Backpacking in
Chile & Argentina

Backpacking in
Chile & Argentina

3rd Edition

Expanded and updated by

Andrew Dixon

with contributions by
Hilary Bradt
Nick Cotton
Clare Hargreaves
John & Christine Myerscough
John Pilkington
and others

BRADT PUBLICATIONS, UK
THE GLOBE PEQUOT PRESS INC, USA

First published in 1980 by Bradt Publications.
Third edition published in 1994 by Bradt Publications,
41 Nortoft Road, Chalfont St Peter, Bucks SL9 0LA, England.
Published in the USA by The Globe Pequot Press Inc, 6 Business Park Road,
PO Box 833, Old Saybrook, Connecticut 06475-0833.

The author and publishers have made every effort to ensure the accuracy of the
information in this book at the time of going to press. However, they cannot accept any
responsibility for any loss, injury or inconvenience resulting
from the use of information contained in this guide.

British Library Cataloguing in Publication Data
A catalogue record for this book is available from the British Library
ISBN 1 898323 04 6

Library of Congress Cataloging-in-Publication Data
A catalog record for this book is available from the Library of Congress
ISBN 1-56440-535-4

Cover photographs
Front: Torres del Paine (Chile) by Janet Cross
Back: Gaucho (Argentina) by Hilary Bradt
Drawings Hilary Bradt
Maps *page vi* Steve Munns *Others* Caroline Crump

Typeset from the author's disc by Patti Taylor, London NW10 1JR
Printed and bound in Great Britain by The Guernsey Press Co Ltd

AUTHORS AND CONTRIBUTORS

Hilary Bradt runs Bradt Publications and leads treks and trips in South America and Madagascar for adventure travel companies.

Nick Cotton spent a year in Chile teaching English and sports. He is the author of several cycle touring books and returned recently to South America to pedal through Tierra del Fuego, Patagonia and southern Chile.

Andrew Dixon spent 18 months in Chile working as an accountant and exploring the Cordillera in his spare time. Originally from Sydney, he now lives in London.

Clare Hargreaves is the author of *Snowfields: the war on cocaine in the Andes* (1992). She has lived and travelled extensively in South America and now works in television.

Christine and John Myerscough are both avid backpackers and photographers. They spent a year exploring Chile, Argentina, Peru, Bolivia and Ecuador.

John Pilkington is an established travel writer with three narrative books under his belt, including *An Englishman in Patagonia*. He also makes travel documentaries for BBC radio.

ACKNOWLEDGEMENTS

Andrew Dixon would like to thank his wife Julia, his secretary Jo Davis, and his hiking companions Herbert and Harvey.

Hilary Bradt thanks all the people who have written to provide information for this new edition: Elizabeth Allison, Rick Ansell, J M Bibby, Sebastian Cooper, Simon Elms, Patrick Frew, Hamish Galpin, Julian Hampson, Denise Heywood, Karin and Matthias Hill, Eric Nijland, Doris Stettler, Patrick Symington, Rob and Jo Withers, and Joanna Wright. Your help was invaluable. Thank you, too, to Dr Jane Wilson Howarth, for checking the health section, and John Pilkington (again) for final checking.

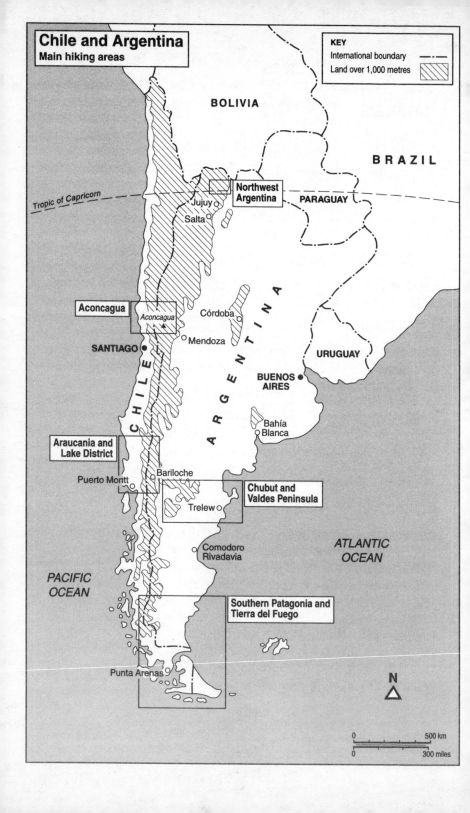

TABLE OF CONTENTS

PREFACE

by Hilary Bradt

Like its predecessor, this edition of *Backpacking in Chile and Argentina* is a *cazuela* of contributors, which is why there is no author's name on the cover. The first edition was written by myself and John Pilkington. We made separate journeys and described different areas and other travellers supplemented our information. The descriptions were updated by Christine and John Myerscough and Clare Hargreaves for the second edition, and now Andrew Dixon, who lived in Chile for a year, has used his experiences along with readers' letters to produce the third edition.

The best walking areas in Chile and Argentina tend to be the Andes which forms the border, so the book wanders between the two countries, moving north to south. The location maps will show you where you are. And if you do not know where you are, don't worry: you are not lost, you are exploring.

Introduction

by Clare Hargreaves

I have too deeply enjoyed the voyage not to recommend any naturalist ... to take all chances and to start on travels by land if possible, if otherwise on a long voyage. He may feel assured he will meet with no difficulties or dangers ... nearly so bad as he beforehand anticipates. He will discover how many truly kind hearted people with whom he never before had, or ever again will have, any further communication who are yet ready to offer him the most disinterested assistance.
Charles Darwin, *The Voyage of the Beagle*

Ever since Darwin penetrated the interior of Chile and Argentina during his voyage in the Beagle in the 1830s, these vast countries on the southern tip of South America have been a source of fascination for travellers.

In his steps followed George Musters, a naval officer who roamed 1400 miles across the windswept Patagonian pampas in the company of a band of Tehuelche Indians; the naturalist William Hudson who, having been shipwrecked on the Atlantic coast, devoted his life to studying the birds of the Rio Negro; and Lady Florence Dixie, the daughter of a Scottish Marquis, who traipsed through southern Argentina with her brother, Lord Queensberry, and a retinue of servants, hunting guanaco and 'wild ostrich' for food.

In the 1980s Patagonia won a place on the literary map through Bruce Chatwin's book, *In Patagonia*, inspired by a piece of South American 'brontosaurus' which adorned his grandmother's drawing room. Other Patagonian titles followed.

Whatever type of landscape or climate turns you on, you can find it in Chile and Argentina. You can swelter on the high parched plateaux around Salta and Jujuy in northwest Argentina or watch elephant seals and killer whales calve off the Valdés Peninsula further south. You can laze in the alpine meadows of the Lakes

District which straddles the border between the two countries, or you can freeze on the fringe of the Antarctic in Tierra del Fuego where the Andes take a final plunge into the sea. The walks in this book take you to all these areas.

If, however, you come here expecting to ride in rickety buses rubbing elbows with brightly clad Indians in bowlers and ponchos, you will be disappointed: the two countries all but eradicated their Indian populations during the War of the Desert at the end of the last century. The majority of people have more in common with Europeans and North Americans than with the native Indian inhabitants.

In consequence, the standard of living in Chile and Argentina is far higher than anywhere else in Latin America. Hotels, restaurants and transport are far more sophisticated than elsewhere — as are their prices. In fact, the only real discomfort you are likely to experience will be the elements — particularly if you opt for a boat trip to the shipwreck-studded rocks of Cape Horn.

In the countryside, however, ancient traditions remain intact. In Argentina you will still see leather-faced gauchos careering across the pampas on horseback who look as if they have leapt straight out of a Wild West movie. And everything they ever told you about Argentinian steak is true: between midday and four in the afternoon any self-respecting Argentine will be found gorging himself with huge hunks of the stuff, a pound at a time, washed down with a few glasses of red Argentinian wine. This is not a good country for vegetarians.

Around the Chilean city of Temuco, you may well encounter some of the last remaining pure-blooded Indians, many of whom still use traditional agricultural methods. As in Darwin's day, Chileans are renowned for their hospitality. You will almost certainly be invited to stay in people's homes, however poor, and be regaled with a *cazuela* (stew) and a bottle of very drinkable Chilean wine. Be careful not to abuse this hospitality.

Walking

Chile and Argentina offer some of the most spectacular walking in South America. Perhaps the best known hiking area is around the magnificent Torres del Paine mountain range in southern Chile. Here you can do an eight day circular walk which offers a superb combination of daisy-filled meadows, snow-capped peaks and vast blue glaciers. Equally fine walking is to be found across the border in Argentina around Mount Fitz Roy, named after the captain of the

Beagle, and on Tierra del Fuego. For those who prefer walking in warmer climes, the Lakes District offers countless hikes past deep-blue lakes, smouldering volcanoes and lush forests. Further north, in northwest Argentina around Salta and Jujuy, is one of the most primitive backpacking areas, where the people and terrain are similar to those of Peru and Bolivia.

Chile and Argentina are a mountaineer's paradise too. Scores have been tantalized by the sheer granite spires of Paine and Fitz Roy or the glaciated peaks of the Cordillera Darwin in Tierra del Fuego. However, since this is primarily a walking, as opposed to a climbing, guide, we only describe climbs that could be done by a reasonably fit walker and do not require specialist expertise. The exception is Aconcagua, which at 6960 metres is the highest mountain in the Americas.

Almost all the trails described in this book are through national parks. They are maintained by the local Club Andino (walking club) and most have *refugios*, or mountain huts, along the route where you can sleep free of charge. Most of the hikes are waymarked with splashes of orange, white or red paint, daubed onto trees, boulders or anything that got in the way of the paintbrush. Normally you have to pay a small fee when you enter a national park, but this never amounts to more than a dollar or two.

Part One

General Information

Chapter One

Preparations

GETTING TO CHILE AND ARGENTINA

As Chile and Argentina have become increasingly popular tourist destinations, fares to both countries have become cheaper and more flexible. Prices vary according to whether or not you travel in the high season (usually December and July) but in the low season you should be able to get a return ticket to Santiago or Buenos Aires from London for around £600.

Because discounted fares are dramatically lower than the 'official' published fares, some general restrictions apply. Normally you must return on a fixed date (validity varies from seven days to 365 days) although one-way tickets and open returns are also available. If you require a visa to visit Argentina (eg: Australians and New Zealanders) you may be required to show a return or onward ticket before this can be obtained. If you purchase your return ticket in either Chile or Argentina expect to pay the 'official' published fare.

Most flights to Chile or Argentina involve a change of plane somewhere and you can normally break the journey for a period of two days to one year, for a charge of approximately $60. From Britain, stopovers in Miami/New York are possible on United Airlines or American Airlines. Within Latin America stopovers are possible en route to either Chile or Argentina, in Bogotá (on Avianca), Carácas (on Viasa), or São Paulo (on Aerolíneas Argentinas and British Airways).

Many airlines offer Open Jaw flights, which allow you to fly to one city and return from another. This can be done using both fixed date fares and yearly open return fares.

If you are a student, teacher or are under 26 you may be eligible for a student fare. However, this may mean even more restrictions.

At the time of writing (October 1996) the cheapest deals from London to Santiago are on KLM and Viasa (around £578 plus APT in the low season). For those wishing to 'fly the flag', British Airways offers a low season fare of £622 plus APT. Best high season fare is with Viasa at £724 plus APT. The most economical low season fares to Buenos Aires are offered by KLM, Aerolíneas Argentinas and BA (£545, £589 and £622 plus APT respectively). As a useful bonus, those booking the £589 flight with Aerolíneas Argentinas are also allowed a 40% discount on internal flights. The cheapest flight to Buenos Aires in the high season is £732 with Aerolíneas Argentinas.

For those wishing to visit both Santiago and Buenos Aires, KLM offers a 'combination' fare to these two capitals of £578 plus £25 for the stopover. Aerolineas Argentinas gives a similar deal at a slightly higher basic fare of £589 (again, all fares are subject to APT).

If you are coming from Europe or North America and are planning to visit other countries in Latin America, then you will find it cheaper to fly in to Carácas, Bogotá, Quito or Lima and to travel on overland. Do not expect to arrive in Chile and Argentina the next day!

Discounted tickets to Chile and Argentina should be booked through agencies specializing in these types of fare. The most knowledgeable in London is Journey Latin America (16 Devonshire Road, Chiswick, London W4, tel 0181 747 3108/8315). Otherwise try Trailfinders (194 Kensington High Street, London W8, tel 0171 938 3939) or STA (main London offices: 86 Old Brompton, SW7, tel 0171 581 4132, 117 Euston Road, NW1, tel 0171 465 0484). STA also has numerous offices around Britain, including Oxford, Cambridge, Bristol, Birmingham and Canterbury.

In North America, try the Student Travel Network or Ladatco (2220 Coray Way, Miami FL33145, tel 1 800 327 6162).

If you are coming from Australia or New Zealand, you can fly to Buenos Aires or to Santiago via Easter Island. Alternatively more regular flights can be obtained by flying via the United States.

Most agencies will offer their own travel insurance, but check to see whether it excludes mountain activities. American Express offers a free (but limited) policy if you buy your tickets with their card.

CLIMATE AND WHEN TO GO

The northern parts of Chile and Argentina have the distinct rainy and dry seasons found in Peru and Bolivia. The dry season is from May to October (the southern hemisphere winter), and the heaviest rain falls from January to March. Further south the climate is temperate with four distinct seasons whose timing is the exact reverse of those in Europe. Spring is usually wet, summer clear and sunny with occasional rainy days, and autumn crisp and cool. As you travel south the summers become cooler and a persistent wind blows, but winters are never really cold, except in the far south.

Northwest Argentina should be hiked in winter (May to October) since the summer rains wash out the trails. But the best times to visit the other areas in this book are late spring, summer or early autumn, that is, November to April. In high summer (January and February) the towns do get a bit crowded for comfort, but at the beginning of March children go back to school and you will have many places completely to yourselves. In April, facilities start to shut down and public transport is reduced, but in July and August everything springs to life again in the Lakes District for the winter sports season. However, only the main roads are kept open at this time, and you will find most of the hikes impassable.

In Patagonia and Tierra del Fuego summer temperatures reach a maximum of 15°C but the average can be taken as lower. The region is notorious for its relentless winds and rain, and at high altitudes it may well snow. One bonus, though, is that in January and February the days are very long and it does not get dark until nearly midnight.

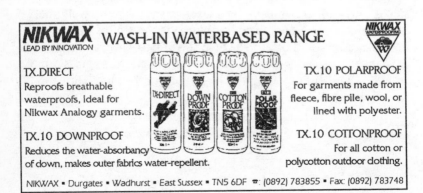

WHAT TO BRING

Apart from backpacking equipment, which is dealt with later, this is obviously a matter of personal preference. However, we advise inexperienced travellers to limit the weight of their packs to 18kg (40lb), and to be particularly careful in the selection of clothes, which must be lightweight but meet the very varied weather conditions.

Clothes

If you are hiking in summer, cold will be not be a problem except in the far south. A woollen sweater will suffice, along with thermal underwear which is lightweight and very warm, and a woollen hat. A duvet (down parka) is useful in Patagonia. Wind is your main enemy, and it is vital to have a windproof anorak (preferably Goretex) which also keeps out the rain.

In the Lakes District in summer you will more often be too hot than too cold, so bring lightweight cotton slacks and shorts, and bear in mind that several layers of thin clothing are more practical than one heavy garment: you can peel off the layers as you warm up. Shorts are comfortable and acceptable away from the main cities. Remember that jeans are heavy to carry, difficult to wash by hand, and take forever to dry. The best trousers are Rohan Bags which are tough, lightweight and dry in no time.

Bring rubber 'flip-flops' to protect your feet in dubious bathrooms, and a swimsuit for those lovely thermal pools.

Other useful items

A small flashlight; credit cards (Visa and Mastercard are the most widely accepted) and international driving licence; student identity card; travel alarm clock; penknife (preferably Swiss Army type); sewing kit; safety pins; large needles and strong thread for tent repairs; scissors; masking tape; Scotch tape (Sellotape); Magic Marker; pencils and ballpoint pens; a small notebook for names and addresses; a large notebook for diary and letters home; plastic bags ('zip-loc' type most useful); a plug for baths and sinks (the flat rubber sort that fits everything); clothes pegs; small scrubbing brush; biodegradable laundry soap/Travel Wash; washing soap (best in a tube); towel; toilet roll; dental floss (excellent for repairs as well as teeth); earplugs (a godsend in noisy hotels and on night buses); high filter suncream; spare glasses and contact lenses; polaroid sunglasses; binoculars; camera; plenty of film; compass; fish-hooks and line; litre water bottle; waterproof matches;

waterproofing for boots; lots and lots of large plastic bags (garbage bags) to cover your pack at night and protect your clothes during the day; whistle; pots, pans and cutlery; strong cord to use as clothes line; plastic screw-top containers (Tuppaware) to carry jam, honey, etc; waterproof map case.

Medicine kit
Insect repellant; water sterilizing tablets or filter; antiseptic cream e.g. Savlon; tampons and contraceptives; Vaseline for cracked heels; dusting powder for feet e.g. Tinaderm, Desenex; adhesive corn pads for blisters; crêpe bandage; Band-Aids (Elastoplast); diarrhoea medication, e.g. Lomotil, Imodium; aspirin and/or paracetamol; oral penicillin; decongestants; 'toothache gel'; travel sickness pills.

Presents
This subject needs reconsidering. For years guide books have been recommending travellers to "bring presents for the friendly locals" without realizing that this is the fastest route to alienation. It is a custom that turns the charming rural children into tiresome beggars who may be angrily shooed away by backpackers. Opportunities for genuine interaction are reduced and cultural differences between the "haves" and "have nots" widened.

That said, Chile and Argentina are different in that there are few indigenous people left (sadly) so local cultures are less fragile. But remember, presents should be given in exchange for services or friendship, not just doled out.

The best presents are those which give an idea of what your home country is like. Most of the rural people you will meet will never have been to your country and probably will never go in their lifetime. Postcards, pins with your country's emblem, stamps from your country, photographs of your family and magazines with lots of pictures always go down well. We found anything to do with Princess Diana or 'Fergie' (pronounced in Argentina as Ferjie) was a real hit too. (The Argentines we met seemed to be far more interested and up to date on Royal gossip than we were.) Comic books, in any language, are much sought after, as are practical gifts such as fish-hooks.

Backpacking equipment
Experienced backpackers will probably already have most of the equipment necessary for a South American trip. Newcomers to backpacking should buy items at a good outdoor equipment shop

where the quality is reliable and salespeople knowledgeable. A list of such shops can be found at the back of walking magazines.

Hiking clothes

If you are going to Patagonia you should equip yourself for plenty of rain and wind. This means taking at least one thick sweater or fleece jacket, a waterproof jacket, and overtrousers. Gore-Tex is a long-standing favourite but there are other, softer, garments such as those made by Paramo which are excellent. In addition you would be strongly advised to take thermal underwear (which can double up as pyjamas), a woollen hat, and gloves (which apart from shielding you from cold are useful protection against thorny trees which you may have to scramble over). We took down-filled jackets and found them a life-saver on cold nights, although opinions vary on their usefulness. They have the advantage of packing up small and being very light, but are useless when it rains. Your everyday trousers must be quick drying — jeans and track suit bottoms should be left at home. Shorts and bathing suit are essential.

Backpack

Rucksack technology has reached an advanced state. A good outdoor shop should advise you on the most suitable for your needs. Berghaus and Karrimor (Britain) and Kelty and Lowe (US) are leaders in the field, and make warm clothing as well. Look for a pack with double zippers which can be secured with a mini padlock. Make sure it has a padded hip belt which shifts the weight from your shoulders onto your hips.

Boots

Comfortable hiking boots with good ankle support are absolutely essential. But if they are leather, make sure you have broken them in before your trip. A number of lightweight boots are now available which are cheaper, do not need breaking in, and in some cases are more waterproof. You should take a pair of old sneakers for fording rivers and for wearing in the evenings.

Sleeping Bag

Although expensive, a down bag is still the warmest and lightest option. However, it is useless if it gets wet, so if you take one you should wrap it in several layers of waterproof covering during the day if it is raining. Synthetically filled bags are getting lighter and warmer all the time, so look around to see what is available. They are also far cheaper. Unless you are going to the far south where you will encounter freezing nights, your main problem is likely to be not keeping warm but keeping cool, so an artificially filled bag (three season) will be adequate. You may also consider taking a bivi-sac cover which adds warmth if you are at high altitudes or far south.

Mat

Some sort of insulation and protection from the cold hard ground is essential. Closed cell 'ensolite' foam pads are the most efficient, providing perfect insulation and tolerable padding even when less than a centimetre thick. They are bulky however. Also recommended is the Therm-a-Rest, a cross between an air mattress and a foam pad, which is lightweight, compact and blissfully comfortable.

Tent

For many of the walks described in this book you can get by without a tent by sleeping in *refugios* (mountain huts). However, a tent will give you greater freedom. It allows you to get away from everybody else and choose your own private camping spot, and can also save you hundreds of dollars on hotel bills.

As with your sleeping bag, weight will be an important factor in determining your choice of tent. Make sure it can withstand tough buffeting from those Patagonian winds. It is worth spending a bit of money to make sure you have the right product which will last. Condensation is also a consideration: most tents are made of permeable nylon which allows moisture to escape, and have a separate fly sheet. A cotton inner tent is more effective in preventing condensation but is heavier. Lightweight tents can be bought in Buenos Aires and Santiago, but their quality is not as high as those available in the US and Europe. In some places you will find tents for hire but these tend to be ancient and to leak.

Light

In summer this will be no problem, particularly down south where it stays light until nearly midnight. At other times of the year you will need some sort of light for your nocturnal doings. Candles can be bought locally (but take care using them in your tent). Otherwise, a headlamp, which frees your hands, is recommended. Bring spare batteries as locally bought ones are sometimes unreliable.

Stove

Campfires are cheerful, warming, and ruinous to the environment. If there is plenty of firewood and a suitable spot for making a fire, go ahead, but generally speaking you should use your stove. The most suitable stoves are those which burn a variety of fuels. The most popular is manufactured by Mountain Safety Research of Seattle, US, also available in Britain. The X-GK stove burns paraffin (kerosene), white gas (stove alcohol), gasoline (called *bencina* in Chile and *nafta* in Argentina) and diesel. It weighs one and a half pounds. The Whisper-lite (same company) is even lighter but does not burn petrol/diesel. Other good stoves available in Britain include the Peak 2 Multifuel stove or the Optimus which burn kerosene (known locally as *parafina azul*). Alternatively you can take a meths burning stove and fuel it with pure alcohol which is readily available and called *solvente para quemar* (at least in Chile).

The cleanest and safest stove is the Bleuet 200 Camping Gaz. But the butane cartridges are forbidden on aeroplanes and they are impossible to buy except in large cities so you will have to stock up and carry them with you.

Backpacking food

Food is a crucial factor in the enjoyment of a holiday. Contrary to what many people might think, meals while you are hiking and camping do not have to consist of crunchy pasta served with a half-hearted tomato sauce. With a bit of imagination and a few local ingredients picked along the way, a camping dinner, while being simple, can be every bit as tasty as it would be back home, if not more so.

If you are backpacking it is best to take dehydrated food which you can supplement with fresh fruit, bread and vegetables. If you are coming from the US or Europe, it is a good idea to buy at least some provisions before you leave as there may be more variety back home. If you are skilful, you can provision yourself with dried food from a supermarket, either back home or in larger towns in Chile or Argentina. Useful items include dried vegetables (peas, peppers, mushrooms, onions etc); porridge oats and/or muesli; dried prawns (we bought them from a Chinese supermarket in London); dried milk; tomato puree in a tube; chocolate; packet soups; pasta, rice and noodles (noodles are by far the best as they take very little time to cook and use minimal fuel); muesli/granola bars; dried fruit such as apricots, prunes and peaches (these can also be nibbled along the way, although beware of taking too much as dried fruit is heavy);

instant custard powder (take from home); tea, coffee and chocolate powder; powdered fruit drinks. If you like jams you will find an incredible variety made from local fruits in the Lakes District, together with excellent honey (*miel*). Make sure you have a leak-proof container to put them in, though. You can buy bread almost everywhere, or resort to the ubiquitous cream cracker. Some people like to take glucose tablets for extra energy on an arduous hike. I always take empty medicine phials or film canisters of pepper and salt.

MONEY

Both Chile and Argentina now use the *peso* $ as their unit of currency. In Argentina hyperinflation in the late 1980s saw the demise of the *austral* which finally became worthless as inflation reached 5000% per annum. President Menem brought in strict anti-inflationary policies in 1991 and stabilized prices by pegging the reintroduced Argentine peso to the US dollar (A$ = US$1) In Chile, at the time of writing (March 1994) C$420 = US$1. Prices in both countries are high compared to other Latin American countries. Argentina is the more expensive of the two.

Beware of exchanging money on the black market; you are more likely to be ripped off than obtain a better rate than those offered by the official exchange houses. Passports are often required at exchange houses and it is advisable to keep your receipts in case you are asked to prove you did not exchange funds on the black market.

US dollars are the easiest form of currency to exchange and they can sometimes be used to purchase goods, though they are accepted more widely in Argentina than Chile. European currencies, including sterling, are of little use.

US dollar travellers cheques are safer to carry than cash, but foreign exchange facilities are rare at banks outside the main towns; you may also be charged up to 5% commission.

You can very easily obtain cash advances on a credit card (Visa or Mastercard) in just about every bank in either country. Check details with your bank before leaving. Credit cards are also widely accepted in restaurants, hotels, bus and train stations and by travel agents.

HEALTH

Before you go

Chile and Argentina have modern medical facilities and excellent doctors. Your preparations for a healthy trip should be the same as for Europe. Very few vaccinations are necessary, but it is advisable to make sure you are up to date on your typhoid, tetanus and polio injections. Yellow fever has now been eradicated in Chile and Argentina and malaria will only be a problem in the extreme northwest of Argentina. If you are spending time there take anti-malaria pills. Phone the Malaria Reference Laboratory in London for the latest advice: 0891 600 350. Hepatitis A is common throughout the continent, so Havrix injections are recommended. Three shots give you a ten-year immunity.

Get a dental check up before you leave and take out medical insurance.

Many drugs, available only on prescription in the UK and US, are sold over the counter in South America, and they are often cheaper, so do not worry about replacing your basic medical supplies there. You are, however, advised to take out your own sterilized needles. In Britain you can buy specially designed Sterile Equipment Packs from Medical Advisory Service for Travellers Abroad (see *Useful Addresses*, page 18).

Remember that prevention is better than cure. Sterilize all water before drinking it, but make sure the water is clear and any dirt particles separated out first. Traditional treating products include tincture of iodine (most effective), Halazone or Sterotab tablets (less good).

Common ailments

Diarrhoea

Although Chile and Argentina are a good deal more hygienic than some of their northern neighbours, you have to face the fact that almost everyone comes down with the trots somewhere in South America. 'Travellers' Diarrhoea' is usually caused by the enterotoxic forms of the bacteria *Escherischia coli* which everyone has in their intestines. The trouble is that each area has its own strain of *E. coli*, and alien strains cause inflammation of the intestine and diarrhoea.

Don't rush off to the pharmacy and stuff yourself with antibiotics at the first signs of *turista*. It is far better to eat nothing, rest and drink plenty of tea or *mate de coca* without milk. Camomile tea (*manzanilla*) is also good. It also helps to sip a solution consisting of salt (¾ teaspoon), baking soda (½ teaspoon), potassium chloride (¼ teaspoon) and sugar or dextrose (4 teaspoons) diluted in half a litre of water. This 'electrolyte replacement' formula is effective and safe and can be made up before leaving home. The diarrhoea should clear up in 24 to 48 hours. If you cannot bear fasting, stick to yoghurt and boiled rice or vegetables.

If you are taking a long bus ride or need a "cork" for another reason, take the traditional "cures" such as Lomotil or Imodium. Bear in mind, however, that these only slow down the workings of the gut; they do not kill the bacteria. For this you need an antibiotic. In 1994 Cyprofloxacin became popular since it only needs a single pill to do the trick, not a course of pills. Try to wait for 24 hours before resorting to antibiotics. If diarrhoea persists and is accompanied by fever and stomach cramps, see a doctor.

Prevention is better than cure. Put crudely, diarrhoea is mostly caused by putting other people's faeces in your mouth. Be scrupulous about washing your hands after using public toilets and before eating, and avoid drinking untreated water or eating any unpeeled or unwashed fruit or vegetables. Eat lots of yoghurt as the bacteria helps combat the bugs in the stomach.

Fever
If you develop a fever you should rest and take aspirin or paracetamol. Bring a supply of ampicillin or tetracycline with you for use as a last resort if you are in a hopelessly inconvenient place, but taking antibiotics without knowing the focus of infection is unwise, so see a doctor before taking antibiotics if at all possible.

Hypothermia
Sometimes referred to as exposure, this is a simple but effective killer. Simply put, it means the body loses heat faster than it can produce it. The combination of wind and wet clothing is lethal, even if the air temperature is well above freezing. Symptoms include exhaustion, shivering, slurred speech, irrational or violent behaviour, dizziness and lethargy. The loss of rationality is particularly dangerous as it means the sufferer often fails to recognize his condition and to take necessary measures. Always carry something waterproof in your backpack, and *get under cover* before becoming thoroughly soaked. To keep your sleeping bag completely dry, carry it inside two plastic bags.

Actually, it is extremely unlikely that people on long hikes will succumb to hypothermia because they carry their weather protection with them. The danger is going on a day hike inadequately equipped, and running into a storm. Always carry waterproofs and a woollen sweater, which is warm even when wet, and turn back if the weather looks threatening.

There are various ways of keeping warm without relying on heavy or expensive clothing. Wear a hat to prevent heat loss from your head. Make sure heat cannot escape from your body through the collar of your windbreaker. Use a scarf or a rollneck sweater. Eat plenty of trail snacks with a high calorie content. Hot drinks have a marvellously warming effect. Have one just before going to sleep (unless you have a weak bladder). Fill your water bottle with hot water, and treat yourself to a 'hotty' at night (but wrap the bottle in a towel first and make sure it is securely sealed).

If a member of your party shows symptoms of hypothermia he/she must be warmed up immediately. Exercise is exhausting and eventually results in worse hypothermia. Make him conserve energy, raise the blood sugar level with food, give hot drinks, and put him in a warmed, dry sleeping bag under cover. If his condition is serious, climb into the bag too and use your body as a radiator.

Injury
Most of the hikes described in this book take you well away from civilization in countries which are sparsely populated anyway. Should you or your companion be injured in one of these remote places, help may not arrive for several days, so hike carefully and avoid taking risks. All backpackers should be conversant with first aid, and be equipped to deal with minor injuries. Carry a book on first aid for mountaineers.

Altitude sickness
Altitude sickness or *soroche* is more likely to affect you on the *altiplano* of Peru or Bolivia than in Chile or Argentina. However, you are almost certain to feel the effects of altitude if you climb Aconcagua, and may do so if you walk in northwest Argentina, where the hikes take you above 2400 metres. It can be avoided by acclimatizing properly, climbing slowly and taking frequent rests. You should also drink plenty of fluids (force them down even if you do not feel like it) and avoid alcohol. The best preventative drug is Diamox which stimulates breathing and reduces the incidence of altitude sickness. It should be taken in a dose of 500mg each morning, starting two days before ascending above 3000 metres and

continuing for a total of one week.

Mild symptoms of altitude sickness are headaches, insomnia, loss of appetite and nausea. If you are suffering from mild symptoms, take aspirin or paracetamol and refrain from climbing higher until symptoms have settled. If however, the symptoms become severe you should descend to a lower altitude *at once*. Severe altitude sickness brought on by a rapid ascent to high altitudes can result in pulmonary oedema (the lungs fill with fluids) or cerebral oedema (fluid collects on the brain). Both can be fatal. Symptoms of severe altitude sickness include splitting headaches, nausea and vomiting, extreme lassitude, stumbling and loss of balance, abnormal speech and behaviour, frothy or blood-stained sputum, progressing to delirium and coma.

Useful addresses

The Berkeley Street Clinic, 32 Berkeley Street, London W1 (near Green Park tube station). Tel 0171 629 6233.

British Airways Travel Clinic and Immunization Service. There are now 36 BA clinics around Britain. To find your nearest one, phone 0171 831 5333. The central London British Airways clinic, at 156 Regent Street, W1, tel 0171 439 9584, also sells travellers' supplies and has a branch of Stanfords travel book and map shop.

Trailfinders Immunization Centre, 19 Kensington High Street, London W8. Tel 0171 938 3999.

Medical Advisory Services for Travellers Abroad (MASTA), Keppel St, London WC1 (tel 0171 631 4408). For a fee, this excellent service will provide an individually tailored Concise Health Brief. This gives up to date information on how to stay healthy in Chile and Argentina, including malaria incidence, inoculations and what to bring. Application forms can be obtained at chemists or by ringing MASTA direct. MASTA also sells basic travel supplies including mosquito nets and Medical Equipment Packs (mentioned above).

SECURITY

When an elderly couple suggested that their driver/guide lock the car before going into a restaurant in Patagonia, he asked, "Why?". There is little casual crime in Chile and Argentina. You should, however, take sensible precautions, especially in cities. Avoid looking like a wealthy tourist: leave your jewellery, dress watch and any other valuables at home. If you carry a bag in addition to your pack, never put it down. Keep it under your arm or over your shoulder. Do not keep valuables in it: not only can it be snatched, but it can be picked, slit or slashed open.

For cash and passports use a neck pouch, money belt or secret inside pocket. A neck pouch is an easy way to carry cash, passports, plane tickets etc, but I find it uncomfortable and I am always worried that someone will try to grab it from my neck. I prefer to use a false pocket sewn into the front of trousers or shorts. Some people favour a 'bum bag' which has the advantage of being able to carry a pocket camera. Whatever you decide to do, always hide an emergency supply of cash.

If your passport is too bulky to carry comfortably and safely, keep handy some other form of identification, such as a driving-licence. It is always a good idea to carry two pieces of identification separately. Then, if your passport is stolen, you can at least prove who you are.

Leaving luggage

Like all travellers, we finish our trips with far more luggage than when we start. Maps accumulate, we buy handicrafts, we collect books, and our packs become quite unpackable. So we have become accustomed to finding a safe place to leave our unwanted baggage while we hike. We have always found a hotel that will keep a bag for us, usually free. Even if they charge, it is not much and it is certainly preferable to lugging it all into the mountains. Bring a lockable bag for this purpose, and make sure it is put somewhere safe, preferably under lock and key. Avoid leaving luggage in hotels frequented by other budget travellers: they are not all as honest as you are, and the policy of claiming your own bag invites theft. If you must use a communal luggage dump, try to chain your bag to something, or at least put your passport number, name and date on it with instructions to give it to no-one else.

Insurance

It is worthwhile getting comprehensive insurance to cover your trip to Chile and Argentina. The knowledge that you can get reimbursed for any precious lost possessions will do much to allay your grief. Most travel agents sell insurance, but read the fine print carefully before you choose. If you do lose something, report it immediately to the local police and insist they give you a *certificado* as proof that you have done so. You will need this when making your claim.

SPANISH

Spanish is not a difficult language so it is worth making the effort to learn the essentials. Your ignorance of the language should not discourage you from making the trip, but we do advise you to learn a few greetings and a basic backpackers' vocabulary, even if you do not aspire to discussing politics and philosophy. You will certainly get more out of your visit.

Both a dictionary and a phrase book are essential. The best dictionary we know of is published by the University of Chicago and based on Latin American Spanish. If you are unable to find a Latin American Spanish dictionary the Larousse American Heritage dictionaries are very good.

You will find there are a number of Spanish words which we have used throughout the book, either because their translation is too long or because it does not convey the same meaning. The most frequent are probably *refugio* (mountain hut or refuge), *guardaparque* (park ranger) and *guardería* (national park office). Note too, the words *ventisquero* and *glaciar* which both mean glacier. Remember these and you will be well along the road. *¡Buena suerte!*

río, arroyo	river, stream
puente	bridge
cerro	mountain
cordillera	mountain range
paso, abra	pass
bahía	bay
quebrada	ravine, gully
lago, laguna	lake
cascada, catarata, salto	waterfall, rapids
ventisquero, glaciar	glacier
témpano	iceberg
estancia	large farm
rancho	small farm, ranch
pampa	meadow, prairie
volcán	volcano
gaucho, huaso	cowboy
campesino	country dweller, peasant

Backpackers' vocabulary

mochila	backpack
mochilero-a	backpacker
andinista	mountaineer
andinismo	mountaineering
refugio	mountain hut
carpa	tent
picada (Arg), *sendero*	path, trail
guardaparque	park ranger
guardería	national park office
portería	national park entrance
acampar	to camp

Useful phrases

¿Adonde va (singular)/*van* (plural)?	Where are you going?
¿De donde viene(n)?	Where are you coming from?
¿De donde es (son)?	Where are you from? (your country)
visitando	visiting
conociendo	getting to know the area
¿Podemos dejar esta bolsa (este paquete) aquí?	May we leave this bag (this package) here?
¿Podemos acampar aquí?	May we camp here?
¿A qué distancia queda?	How far is it?
¿Puede ayudarme?	Can you help me?
Donde está el camino por...	Where is the path to...

Dialects, accents, and colloquial Spanish

Chileans and Argentines have the infuriating habit of not speaking Spanish the way one learnt it at school/evening class. The Chilean version is perhaps the hardest to understand, mainly because they speak it so quickly. However in both countries you will notice the consonant *s* being dropped with much abandon, especially when it occurs at the end of a word, which makes it rather difficult to know whether things are singular or plural. In Argentina, the confusion is compounded by a tendency to pronounce the consonants *ll* and *y* like the *si* in inva*si*on, and by an inclination to use the old Spanish word *vos* instead of the second person singular *tu*.

Ciao is commonly used in both countries to say hello or goodbye and the Argentine males often refer to each other as *che* or *flaco*. In addition, Chileans commonly add the diminutives *ito* or *ita* to the ends of words, and you will even hear *ciaoito*.

Chapter Two

Travelling and living

TRANSPORT

I asked the sleeping car attendant what was up. The tracks, he said.
Paul Theroux *The Old Patagonian Express.*

Chile and Argentina are big places, with lots of empty space. In fact you could drop the whole of Western Europe on the two countries and still have thousands of acres round the edge. This means that getting from one place to another by road or rail will take not hours but days. Some sample distances: Arica to Puerto Montt, 2900 kilometres; Buenos Aires to Ushuaia, 3200 kilometres; Salta (northwest Argentina) to Ushuaia, 4700 kilometres.

Air

Both Chile and Argentina have excellent, reasonably priced domestic air services. In Chile they are provided by the airlines LanChile and Ladeco and Saba, in Argentina by Aerolíneas Argentinas, Austral LAPA, CATA, Transporte Aéreo Neugén (TAN) and LAER. In the holiday months of January and February these get very full so you need to book well in advance.

In addition, the Argentine Air Force has an airline of its own, Líneas Aéreas del Estado (LADE). If you want to go somewhere where the civil airlines do not go, such as Calafate, the chances are that you can go with LADE: an experience not to be missed, especially as it is sometimes actually cheaper than going by bus. Again, you will need to book well in advance as planes get very full. If you are told a flight is full, however, it is always worth turning up at the airport on the off-chance.

If you are thinking of doing a lot of your travelling by air, it is certainly worth considering buying an air pass. These vary in price according to your route and can only be bought outside the country.

LanChile offer a 21-day pass for travel between Arica and Puerto Montt for $250, while Aerolíneas and Austral offer a 30-day pass with four coupons for $450. Additional coupons cost $120. Ladaico, Chile's other airline, do a similarly priced pass. For up to date details of LanChile's passes phone (London) 0171 730 2128.

Buses

Long distance buses in Chile and Argentina are comparable to those in North America, and better than many in Europe. Fast, reliable, comfortable, they could hardly be more different from the rustic vehicles of the Andean countries further north. As you might expect, they are not cheap, particulary in Argentina. The trip from Buenos Aires to Bariloche, for example, costs about US $70 — only marginally less than the airfare. In spite of this, buses are very popular, and during the main holiday period of January and February may be booked up weeks in advance.

Trains

A cheap and civilized way to travel, provided you have the time, is by train. Both Chile and Argentina have extensive railway systems, stretches of which have become famous through Paul Theroux's *The Old Patagonian Express*. Chile has 10,100 kilometres of line, stretching from Iquique near the Peruvian border to Puerto Montt (although the line north of Santiago is now closed). Argentina's network is bigger still, stretching from La Quiaca on the Bolivian border to Esquel/Bariloche. However neither system goes south of the Lakes District. On the Chilean side this is for the very good reason that the mountains and fjords made railways impossible to build. In Argentina the extreme sparsity of settlement in the vast pampas of the south meant that railways were never an economic proposition, except for a few special lines such as that connecting the Río Turbío coal mines with the sea.

Apart from being cheaper than buses, trains often give better views of landscape and wildlife. If you have 18 hours to spare, we highly recommend the overnight journey between Puerto Montt and Santiago. It is like travelling inside an antique — which is what the train is, having been built by the Germans in 1926. For around $40 you can sleep in a spacious velvet-lined bed with starched white sheets having enjoyed a perfectly edible (but expensive) dinner in the dining car with superb views of Volcán Osorno. The only drawback is that timetables do tend to be very elastic and the ageing hardware of track and rolling stock are subject to all kinds of unlikely mishaps.

NOTE: In March 1993, the Argentine government withdrew funding from the national railways. Responsibiity for the services now lies with the provinces. In many cases, the provinces have been unable to maintain the tracks and rolling stock and have therefore either had to cancel or reduce the number of services.

Hitchhiking

If you have got time to spare, hitchhiking will more than repay the effort. Both Chile and Argentina have good road systems and, more to the point, plentiful traffic, particularly in the summer months. Hitchhiking is common and accepted on all the main routes, but on the back roads of Patagonia and Tierra del Fuego is recommended only for the very patient. John once waited two days for a lift here. Hilary once waited two and a half days.

Car hire

This is a very expensive means of transport, particulary in Chile where you are not likely to want to return to where you hired the car from. In addition, it is not possible to take a hire car across the border.

ACCOMMODATION

Accommodation, like transport, has more in common with Europe or North America than with the rest of Latin America. This means that water usually comes out of taps, and toilets generally work in the manner you are accustomed to. It also means that, as in Europe and North America, the price of accommodation has risen steeply in recent years. This is especially true of Argentina where prices match or exceed European ones.

In both countries you will come across a bewildering variety of names to describe a place where you can sleep: *hotel, hostería, hospedaje, residencial, pensión*. On the whole, budget travellers will want to opt for the latter three or get a room in a private house, although *hoteles* are found in all price ranges. Occasionally you may decide to splash out on a really nice hotel, such as the one in the Torres del Paine National Park, in Chilean Patagonia.

In Chile, where you will find many places run by dear old ladies of German ancestry, breakfast is often included in the price of the room. In Argentina it is almost always extra. In both countries prices rise noticeably as you move south, and are at their most exorbitant in the fashionable tourist resorts such as Bariloche and

San Martín de los Andes.

The *South American Handbook* has up-to-date information on accommodation of all kinds (see *Bibliography*).

LOCAL DISHES AND WINES

Chile

Seafood is the speciality here and the variety is enormous. Our best recommendation is to try everything. Conger eel (*congrio*) is probably the most common type of fish; don't be put off by the fact that it's an eel. Hilary recommends you watch out for *erizos* or sea urchins as she says she has tasted nothing more disgusting; I found them delicious. A seafood dish that never fails to be less than scrumptious is *chupe de mariscos*, a thick shellfish soup often topped with cheese.

Of non-seafood dishes perhaps the most typical is *cazuela de ave* a nutritious stew containing large chunks of chicken, potatoes, rice and maybe onions and green peppers. Also tasty are *empanadas*, turnovers or pasties with raisins, olives, meat, onions and peppers inside.

Other Chilean dishes include:

locos	abalones (giant shellfish)
caldillo de congrio	conger eel soup
paila chonchi	bouillabaisse or fish stew
ostras	oysters
mejillones or *cholgas*	mussels
almejas	clams
camarones	shrimp
pastel de choclo	casserole of meat, onions and olives with maize-meal mash on top
prieta	blood sausage stuffed with cabbage leaves
parillada de mariscos	grilled mixed seafood
curanto	typical Chilote stew of seafood, chicken, potatoes, beef, vegetables and pork

In Punta Arenas and Tierra del Fuego you should definitely try southern king crab (*centolla*). This enormous creature, may measure a metre from leg to leg and weigh as much as two kilograms.

Chilean wines are excellent and are rapidly gaining international recognition. It is one of the few places in the world where the vines have not been affected by *phyllexora*, the disease that wiped out acres of vine in Europe. Among the best *bodegas* are Cousiño Macul, Concha y Toro, Santa Carolina, Undurraga, San Pedro and Santa Elena. You can see the complete spectrum of Chilean wines, and indulge in some free tasting, at the *enoteca* (wine 'library') in the mountains overlooking Santiago.

Argentina

The basis of the Argentine diet is *asado*: barbecued beef or lamb. No fiesta or family gathering is complete without an *asado*, and even street workers regularly set up their charcoal fires for a lunchtime steak. Other popular dishes include:

puchero	pot-au-feu consisting of meat, maize, potatoes and squash
carbonada	ground beef with onions and tomatoes
churrasco	thick cut beef steak
parrillada	mixed grill
milanesa	wienerschnitzel
bife de chorizo	rump steak
locro	a thick soup of maize, white beans, meat, pumpkin and herbs
fiambre and *matambre*	fancy cold-cuts, especially good for picnics.

A great treat is *dulce de leche*, a sort of liquid fudge spread which can be eaten with bread and cheese or on its own. Completely heavenly. Chile has an equivalent product but calls it *manjar blanco*. Other typical sweets include *dulce de membrillo* (quince jelly), *dulce de batata* (sweet potato preserve), and *dulce de zapallo* (pumpkin in syrup).

Unusually for South America, Argentine salads are excellent and generally safe. And lovers of Italian food will be pleased to know that the pizzas of Buenos Aires are among the best in the world.

Argentine red wine (*vino tinto*) is a standard accompaniment to any meat dish. Although drunk regularly by all Argentines, it is rarely taken in large quantities, and often mixed with mineral water to make a refreshing long drink. White wine (*vino blanco*) is good but less common. Most Argentine wine comes from the provinces of Mendoza and San Juan, where it is produced in huge *bodegas* or processing plants. The historic Bodega de Arizú in Mendoza offers a fascinating tour, with free samples of course.

Eating wild

Devotees of wild food will be in their seventh heaven here. The temperate zones of South America have such an abundance of edible berries, greenery, fungi, eggs and sea food that even people who have never sampled the fruits of the trail before will probably succumb to temptation.

As in any country, you should not eat wild food until you have positively identified it. Here are a few of the tastier possibilities.

Berries

The *calafate* berry, or **barberry**, grows in great profusion in Patagonia and Tierra del Fuego and tastes similar to the blackcurrant or blueberry. In Patagonia there is an old saying *'Quien come el calafate vuelve por más'* (Whoever eats the *calafate* berry will come back for more) which just shows how addictive this berry — or the landscape — can be. The *calafate* grows on spiny bushes and ripens between January and March. Its dark purple juice stains the lips and tongue a beautiful mauve. It also happens to be a good laxative. As the berries are full of pips it is best to gather a quantity and stew them in a little water and sugar. Then you can strain off the juice (we used some spare mosquito netting) and you will have a thick syrup which will keep for a few days and can be diluted as you need it. It is especially good poured over the morning's porridge, or as dessert with yogurt or custard.

Calafate

The **wild strawberry or rainberry** grows abundantly in Tierra del Fuego. Being composed of lots of tiny lumps, it looks like a small raspberry and tends to grow in tree mould or moss. Delicious with sugar and cream.

The **diddle-dee berry** (*sepisa*), found in many parts of Tierra del Fuego, is rather bland compared with the rainberry. There are two types: bright red or black.

The **blackcurrant** grows extensively in Tierra del Fuego and Patagonia. But it is unwise to eat a huge quantity as it is an effective laxative.

Blackberry (*mora*) bushes were introduced to Chile by the early settlers as hedging, and they soon spread throughout the Lakes

District. You can stuff your face with blackberries in this area in March and April.

The **murta berry** has a sweet, slightly perfumed flavour and makes delicious jam. If you visit the Lakes District around Easter you will almost certainly see people at the roadside selling buckets of these small, red berries. You will find them growing wild, among other places, on the lower slopes of Volcán Osorno.

Greenery

If you are accustomed to eating sorrel, wild garlic, wild celery, cress or mint, at home, you can do so here. You can also eat the inner stem of the tussock grass or the tangy leaves of the scurvy grass.

Wild celery and cress grow in damp areas, sorrel in sunny meadows and mint everywhere. Try mint tea.

Fungi

The climate of southern Chile and Argentina seems to be ideal for fungi. Never have we seen so many varieties — tantalizing if you do not know what they all are. The ones we recognized were field mushrooms, giant puffballs, shaggy ink caps and coral mushrooms. If you are a mushroom enthusiast we strongly recommend that you bring your field guide. Most of the fungi in this part of the world are the same as those you find in Europe or North America.

We can particularly recommend the giant puffballs that are common in Torres del Paine National Park. We ate them in a variety of ways: fried in sardine oil, mixed with soup, and thinly sliced and dried in the sun, after which they were as crunchy and tasty as potato crisps.

Seafood

Here we include river and lake trout, if you are lucky or skilful enough to catch one. Chile and Argentina offer some of the best trout fishing in the world, and few backpackers can pass through areas such as the Lakes District without being infected by the fishing bug. We tried the local method, using bait or lures and a tin can for casting. We had many bites, but most of the trout got away. We had not anticipated the size and strength of these monsters.

The type of sea food which stays still for the picking is less frustrating. Mussels top our list. In Tierra del Fuego National Park there are extensive mussel beds, but you will find them in other places too. Mussels should be gathered at low tide, preferably on the lee shore where they are less concerned with pearl production. If you are heading towards a known mussel bed, it is worth indulging yourself by packing along a bottle of white wine for *moules marinières*. Just steam the mussels in a little wine for about ten minutes or until they open. If you can find some wild garlic, that is even better.

Clams are harder to find but well worth the effort. Empty clam shells on a sandy beach should be evidence enough to encourage you to look for their holes. They live four to six inches below the surface and can be dug out with a stick or tentpole. They can then be steamed like mussels.

If, amazingly, you have acquired the taste for sea urchins, you can eat their orange roe raw or steamed, using a mussel shell as a container and setting it on a bed of seaweed.

All crabs are edible. You are unlikely to catch a king crab (*centolla*), though people do manage to fish them from shallow water in the Río Grande area of Tierra del Fuego. Better settle for one of the smaller varieties if you can find them.

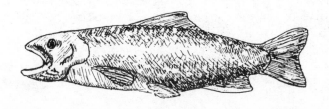

NATURAL HISTORY
by Hilary Bradt

These goslings are black and white and have feathers over their whole body of the same size and fashion, and they do not fly, and live on fish... The sea wolves have a head like that of a calf and small round ears. They have large teeth and no legs, but feet attached to their body resembling a human hand. And they had nails on these feet and skin between the toes like the gosling. And if they could have run they would have been truly fierce and cruel; but they do not leave the water, where they swim wondrously and live on fish.
Diary entry by Pigafetta during Magellan's voyage down the Patagonian coast, 1520.

To the sixteenth century Portuguese the penguin and sealion were animals 'the like of which no Christian man had e'er set eyes on' and to twentieth century travellers they are still fascinating, if more familiar. Inland there is also much to interest backpackers. The flora and fauna you are most likely to come across in the Lakes District, Patagonia and Tierra del Fuego are described below.

Vegetation
The Andean foothills are heavily forested. The genus *Nothofagus* (also found in New Zealand) has several species here, the most common of which is the southern (false) **beech**, or *lenga* (*N. pumilio*), a deciduous tree with a copper tinge to the leaves. Also abundant is the tall evergreen **coihue** (*N. dombeyi*). In the Lakes District you will see beautiful *arrayanes* with their peeling red bark; Walt Disney set *Bambi* amongst these fairytale trees.

There used to be huge stands of the native **monkey puzzle** tree (*Araucaria araucana*) throughout southern Chile. They are now confined mostly to the Lakes District, though you may see scattered examples elsewhere.

There are many small flowering trees and bushes, such as the aptly named fire bush with its red blossoms, and the *calafate* bush (box-leaved barberry) with its yellow flowers and edible berries. Fuschia are also common. Chile's national flower is the *copihue*, characterized by the deep pink elongated bell-shaped flowers on a creeper which clings to the larger trees and bushes. You can see it on Cerro Ñielol, near Temuco. In spring the meadows are a mass of colour: wild gentian, daisies, vetch, and the larger lupins and fragrant sweet maidens. Look out also for the lovely *ourisia*, which grows near waterfalls, and the yellow orchid (*Gavileo lutia*).

In the temperate rain forests of the south there are over 400 species of moss. I will not attempt to describe them.

Birds

I have only space here to point out some of the more interesting or conspicuous birds, so keen bird-watchers should get hold of a South American field guide (see *Bibliography*).

Ashy-headed goose

Ruddy-headed goose

Waterfowl are the most noticeable group. You will come across beautiful geese, including the **ashy-headed goose** and the **ruddy-headed goose**, and a variety of ducks, some sporting plastic-looking blue bills. The **Andean** or **ruddy duck** is the most common. You will probably see **torrent ducks** by fast flowing rivers. These attractive small ducks feed on stonefly larvae which can only exist in highly oxygenated water, hence the birds' reckless dives into the rushing torrents. **Black-necked swans** are also frequently seen.

In the forests and plains there are many conspicuous birds. The ubiquitous **buff-necked ibis**, or *bandurria*, inhabits marshy ground and feeds on small aquatic creatures. Its dramatically marked black and grey wings and loud alarm call are unmistakable. The **southern lapwing**, or *tero*, is equally noisy. The **tinamou**, or *martineta*, scurries about the plains wearing a ridiculous pointed hat, and is much prized as a game bird. Look out too for the **Chilean flicker** or *piteo*, the **Magellanic woodpecker**, and the tiny **Austral pygmy**

Spine-tail

Crested tinamou (martineta)

owl (known locally as a *chuncho*).

The tiny **spine-tail** is a forest dweller with strong views about its territorial rights. You will hear its noisy calls before you see the orange and brown bird with its strange spiky tail.

In Tierra del Fuego there are two members of bird families normally associated with tropical climates: hummingbirds and parrots. The Chilean **fire-crowned hummingbird** is brilliant green with an iridescent red crown, and the **Austral parakeet**, the only parrot found at this latitude, is dark green with a reddish belly and tail. In *araucaria* forests lives the **slender-billed parakeet** which uses its specially adapted beak to probe for pinenuts in the monkey puzzle trees. Although the fire-crowned hummingbird is the most southerly, there are six other species of hummingbird in Chile and Argentina including the dove-sized **giant hummingbird**.

Birds of prey are quite common, the largest being the **Chilean eagle** or grey-backed buzzard which feeds on rodents and small birds. **Ospreys** are summer visitors, and the small **red-tailed buzzard** is often seen. Carrion eaters include **caracaras** and **turkey vultures** which hang around sheep stations. But the most impressive carrion eater is the world's largest, the **Andean condor**. This huge bird is quite common in the southern Andes, and can be recognized in flight by its white fluffy neck ruff and the 'fingering' of the primary wing feathers. The Andean condor has the largest wing area of any bird, but the three metre span is not as great that of the **wandering albatross** which has the largest wing span of all. These marvellous birds are occasionally seen near the shore during their wanderings in the southern seas. You may also see the **great skua**, which resembles a large brown gull. They are opportunists and scavengers, ever ready to grab an egg or young bird. Skuas are fiercely territorial: woe betide the unprotected head of the backpacker who inadvertently wanders near a skua nest!

The most distinctive large bird is the flightless **rhea**, South America's version of the ostrich. Darwin's rhea, the species inhabiting the southern part of the continent, is smaller than the ones found further north. Female rheas are thoroughly liberated, playing no part in the raising of their family. The male has the responsibility of mating with a variety of

Rhea

females, collecting the twenty or so eggs that they lay haphazardly around his chosen nest site, incubating them entirely unaided, and then caring for the lively chicks.

The penguin found around the southern coast is the **Magellanic** or 'Jackass' **penguin** (not the true Jackass which is found only in South Africa, but they have the same donkey-like bray). They nest in burrows near the shore, and when alarmed run on all fours, using their flippers as an extra pair of legs and achieving remarkable speeds with no apparent concern for physical safety. Once in the shelter of their burrows they glare at you out of first one eye, then the other, wagging their heads from side to side. Of all the penguin species they are the least dignified.

Land mammals

There are very few land mammals of any size in this part of South America, the largest indigenous species being the **guanaco**. This wild cousin of the domesticated llama is a slender, elegant animal, golden brown in colour fading to white on the belly and inner legs. Guanacos live in family groups with one male guarding from four to 12 females. The young, called *chulengos*, are adorable animals and often kept as pets, but they tend to become vicious as they grow up. Like all members of the llama family, guanacos are very inquisitive and give passing backpackers their full attention.

Two species of fox can be found in Chile and Argentina. The small grey **Patagonian fox** is common throughout the region and has been introduced into Tierra del Fuego, threatening the habitat of the rarer and much larger Fuegian fox or **Andean wolf**, which has reddish tints to its grey coat.

Rodents are plentiful, the most interesting being the **mara** or Patagonian hare. These strange inhabitants of the Patagonian plains look as though they were designed by a committee. They have box-like faces, long ears, spindly legs and a horizontal white stripe across their bottoms. Despite the name they are not true hares, being related to another member of the rodent family, the agouti.

The seal family

Seals evolved some 30 million years ago, and can be divided into two groups: *Otariidae*, or eared seals, descended from a bear-like animal; and *Phocidae*, true seals, whose ancestors were otter-like carnivores. Seals are far more at home in the sea than on land, and all species share special adaptive features: hind limbs have evolved into tail-like appendages, forelimbs into flippers, and the seals are insulated from the cold Antarctic seas by five centimetres or more of blubber beneath their skin.

All South Atlantic seals share the same seasonal timetable. In spring the bulls arrive on shore to establish their territories; then the cows join them, and those that are pregnant give birth after a few days. As soon as the pups are independent the parents return to the sea to feed, and come back to shore in the autumn again to moult. This accomplished, they leave until the following spring.

In Chile and Argentina you may see southern sealions, fur seals and elephant seals.

Southern sealions

Southern sealions

Sealions are eared seals and their small external ears are clearly visible. They are much more mobile on land than true seals, being able to rotate their rear flippers sideways to propel their bodies forward. Sealions can move quite fast in this manner: something to remember if you meet an angry bull. A full-grown bull southern sealion is much larger and more impressive than his northern cousin, the Californian sealion. This massive animal is well over two metres in length, and weighs up to half a ton. His enormous neck is adorned with a shaggy mane: hence the name sealion, which also refers to his roar. The elegant limpid-eyed females that make up his harem weigh only a quarter of his great bulk, but then they expend less energy.   From the time he comes ashore in December to when he leaves in March, the bull sealion neither eats nor sleeps for more than a few minutes at a time. Guarding his harem is a full time job.

The black furry pups are born in early January. They are not fully weaned for six months, but the females return to the sea for feeding before this time, leaving a nursery or 'pod' of pups to gain safety in numbers. In fact they have few land predators, and the high juvenile mortality rate is largely through the clumsy actions of fighting males.

Fur seals

Only their golden brown fur and upturned noses distinguish fur seals from sealions. This luxurious coat almost led to their extinction, but now they are fully protected and their numbers are increasing. The fur seal has two layers of fur: a soft dense undercoat, and an outer layer of coarse hair which traps bubbles of air to increase insulation. In fact, fur seals often seem to get too hot, and you will see them wave their flippers around in an attempt to cool off. There are marvellous 'rookeries' of these animals on Península Valdés. Try to visit in January when there is plenty of action; you will hardly be able to tear yourself away.

Elephant seals

These massive animals can measure as much as six metres and weigh around three tons (the record is nearly seven metres long — 22½ feet — and four tons). The bull elephant seal has an elongated nose which can be inflated and extended, although only bulls in rut give this spectacular display. Normally they content themselves with letting it overhang their mouths as they roar a warning to another bull or a tiresome human.

Elephant seal

Although you could never call a female elephant seal elegant, they have endearingly placid expressions, with huge dark eyes designed for deep sea fishing. They are half the size of the bulls, with no 'trunk'.

These true seals have great difficulty heaving themselves overland since their hind limbs are useless for propulsion. Consequently both bulls and cows are loathe to stir themselves and can be easily approached (where permitted), although they may give vent to their annoyance by emitting a belching roar. An angry bull adds to the effect by rearing upright so that only his tail end remains on the ground. They have remarkably supple spines and can even touch their head with their tails. When forced to move they undulate along the beach like giant maggots.

Elephant seals come ashore for two periods during the year. The males arrive in late August or September and immediately start establishing territories. Their fights are impressive, each contestant slashing the other with its canine teeth. They bang their chests together so that fat ripples down their bodies like heavyweight wrestlers. Once territories are established the females arrive, and soon give birth. Unlike sealions, which keep their puppy fur for a year, these babies moult after a month. They are able to start swimming and fending for themselves soon after moulting is finished but may continue to suckle for a few more weeks. Elephant seal milk is reputedly the richest in the world, being 80 per cent fat.

Like sealions, bull elephant seals do not eat during this period on shore. Once the parents are relieved of the cares of mating and child rearing, they return to the sea to feed, coming back in the autumn to moult. They lie morosely on the beach, looking like sun-burned tourists with their skin hanging off in strips, and do little else but wallow in the mud and scratch. The onlooker has an excellent chance at this season to observe the transformation of their forelimbs from ugly flippers to nimble 'hands', able to deal with a nasty itch as daintily as a dowager.

Until the arrival of man, elephant seals had but one enemy: the killer whale. When sealers found that one elephant seal would yield 80 gallons of oil their future was threatened, but under protection their numbers are now recovering.

Visitors with a special interest in natural history should contact the Argentine Wildlife Foundation (Fundación Vida Silvestre Argentina), Defensa 245/251, Buenos Aires. The Foundation publishes articles on wildlife and sponsors lectures and other educational programmes.

GAUCHOS AND HUASOS
by Hilary Bradt

The horse played the same role in the shaping of Chile and Argentina as it did in the American West. The vast Argentine pampas were tamed by gauchos riding Spanish horses, and these cowboys played a decisive part in the bitter internal struggles following independence.

Gauchos were usually of Spanish/Indian descent, and the name derives from a Quechua word meaning 'orphan' or 'abandoned one'. It was a lonely life on the pampas, and the gauchos were fiercely independent men whose home was the open range. They lived almost entirely on beef, which they roasted in an open pit and then washed down with draughts of *yerba mate*, a herb tea. They drank heavily of *aguardiente* (sugar brandy) and spent much of their free time playing cards. The main tools of their trade were *boleadoras* or *bolas*, stones attached to cords which they used to bring cattle down from a distance by entangling them around their legs. Their dress, still worn by their descendants today, included a thick woollen poncho over the shoulders, a *rastra* (a broad belt studied with silver coins) around the waist, and long, pleated trousers called *bombachas* which were gathered at the ankles and covered the tops of their high leather boots. Like the North American cowboy, the gaucho became something of a folk hero, symbolizing the freedom and pioneer spirit of nineteenth century Argentina. He was immortalized in Jose Hernandez' epic poem, *Martin Fierro*.

The Chilean huaso lacked the glamour of the gaucho. This may be because his historic role was more utilitarian and had to do with herding cattle rather than fighting wars, or perhaps because the limited space west of the Andes confined the spirit of these men and failed to ignite the proud arrogance which symbolizes the Argentine gaucho. Darwin noted that "The gaucho may be a cut-throat but he is a gentleman; the huaso is an ordinary vulgar fellow".

Rodeos

The rodeo, in some ways the Southern Cone's equivalent of the Spanish bullfight, is an important part of the summer calendar in both Chile and Argentina. It differs widely between the two countries.

Chilean rodeos feature only one contest. An oval arena is divided lengthways by a fence, forming a half moon or *medialuna*. A section of the outer fence is padded, and the contest is between two huasos and a steer. The animal is driven round the *medialuna* by one huaso riding close to its tail and the other at its side keeping it near the fence. After making a complete circuit, the steer is pinned against the padded section by one rider, turned around by the other, and driven out of the arena. It is all rather boring since points are given on technical details which escape the uninformed viewer. The huasos are fine-looking men wearing short striped ponchos (*chamantas*) and flat-topped sombreros. Their wicked looking spurs have enormous sharpened rowels.

Argentine rodeos have a varied programme and are similar in many ways to those in North America. The contests are undoubtedly very cruel, but are a reflection of life on the pampas where animals must be quickly tamed or subdued. There are various roping contests and bucking broncos, and once we watched a fascinating exhibition of wild horse breaking. The animal was driven into the ring and lassoed by a mounted gaucho, who threw it to the ground and blindfolded it before tying its front legs. A rawhide bit was put in its mouth, and it was urged to its feet and saddled. The rope securing it to the gaucho's horse was shortened so that the trembling animal stood next to the other horse, and the hobble was removed. The gaucho then mounted his own horse and in one movement transferred to the other and removed the restraining rope and blindfold. The wild horse leapt away, bucking furiously, but was gradually brought to hand and learned to accept the rider's control. Ten minutes after being driven into the ring it was wheeling and turning to the gaucho's command, then came quietly to a standstill.

The most important rodeo in Argentina is held in May at Ayacucho, not far from La Plata. Gauchos and horses representing different parts of the country parade. This has to be seen to be believed. The horses are adorned with solid silver bridles with gold inlay, and silver stirrups. Some tack is made from decoratively twisted rawhide, with circular stirrups allowing just a toehold. The gauchos are impeccably dressed in embroidered waistcoats, with jewel-studded daggers in their belts. This memorable three day affair finishes with a free-for-all *asado* and much wine drinking.

CHILE FACTBOX

Area: 760,000 square kilometres

Length: 4329 kilometres.

Average width: 180 kilometres.

Coastline: 4500 kilometres.

Population: 13.4 million

Mean monthly temperatures

Arica: 16°C (July) to 22°C (January)
Santiago: 9°C (June) to 20°C (January)
Punta Arenas: 2°C (July) to 11°C (January)

Public holidays

Ist January   New Year's Day
Holy Thursday
Good Friday
Ist May   Labour Day
21st May   Navy Day
I5th August   Assumption
I8th September   Independence Day
I9th September   Army Day
12th October   Discovery of America
1st November   All Saints Day
8th December   Immaculate Conception
25th December   Christmas Day

Chapter Four

Chile: essential facts

Introduction

Embracing almost 40 degrees of latitude (or over 70 if you include its claim to part of Antarctica) Chile encompasses more climates, landscapes and ways of life than any other country of its size in the world. Your impressions will depend very much on which part you visit. Chile is over 4300 kilometres long and averages only 180 kilometres in width. To the west is the Pacific ocean and to the east the Andes, with many peaks over 6000 metres (the highest mountain chain outside the Himalayas), spanning the border with Argentina.

From north to south the country falls into five sharply contrasted zones:

1.   The northern desert with its huge deposits of nitrate and copper, occasional oases and the port of Antofagasta.
2.   The semi-desert with its irrigated valleys. The main centre here is La Serena.
3.   The heartland where most of Chile's population live. Great farms and vineyards cover this area which is exceptionally beautiful. It also includes the country's three largest cities: Santiago, Valparaíso and Concepción.
4.   The area of forests, mountains and lakes between Concepción and Puerto Montt, known as the Lakes District. Main centres are Temuco, Valdivia and Puerto Montt.
5.   The islands, forests, fjords, mountains and glaciers between Puerto Montt and Cape Horn. This sparsely populated area offers some of the country's finest and wildest scenery.

Another reason why you can expect varying impressions in different parts of the country is the people. Apart from the few Indians you may meet around Temuco, your most likely acquaintances, other than *mestizos* (people of mixed blood), will be the people of German origin in the Lakes District, and Yugoslavs or British in the far south. These are descendants of 19th century immigrants and many still speak their mother tongue. (This may help if you do not speak Spanish.) Their influence can also been seen in the appearance of the towns and villages.

Visas

Chile is one of the most liberal countries in South America when it comes to entry requirements. It does not require visas of visitors from Western Europe, North America or Australia, unless they are on business. (But French and New Zealand passport holders do require a visa.) On entering the country you will be given a tourist card, valid for 90 days and renewable for up to another 90 days. The renewal process is a law unto itself and usually involves two visits to the Ministerio de Relaciones Exteriores. Far better to pop across the Argentine border and re-enter. I met someone who had been doing this for three years. Keep your tourist card in a safe place, preferably in your passport, as without it there will be an enormous fuss when you try to leave.

Visas allowing you to work can only be obtained if you have an employment contract. Employers are reluctant to employ foreigners without the proper work papers and, if they do, they will usually not be offering a very high wage.

Note that it is forbidden to bring fresh fruit or vegetables, dairy products or fresh meat into Chile.

SANTIAGO
Introduction
Opinions are divided on Chile's capital city: some people love it, some hate it. Most agree that the architecture is singularly uninspiring but the setting magnificent (when the smog doesn't obscure the view of the Andes). It is also a huge metropolis (fourth largest after Rio, São Paulo and Buenos Aires) and those who do not like big cities will probably pass on as quickly as they can.

Santiago lies in a valley between the Andes (commonly referred to as the *cordillera*) and a lower coastal range. Whilst the *cordillera* provides a magnificent backdrop, it unfortunately traps the pollution caused principally by the diesel buses and unrestricted industries. Present smog levels regularly rival those of Los Angeles and Mexico City. Restrictions have been imposed banning cars and buses from driving through the city centre on certain days. Fortunately, you do not have to travel far in any direction to find fresh air. To escape, the capital's inhabitants (the *Santiaguinos*) head for the ski resorts in winter and to Viña del Mar in the summer.

In summer, the climate is hot and dry with temperatures often reaching 30°C. To compensate, the winters are cool and wet.

In spite of its size Santiago strikes you immediately as a friendly place. The pace of life is less frenetic than in most Latin American capitals, and people have time to stop and chat.

Things to do
To the north of the city, located by the Mapocho river, is the Central Market, a wrought iron structure made in England. Here you will find plenty of interesting foodstuffs and seafood, including the huge *congrios* (conger eels) which feature on most restaurant menus. Heading east, beside the river, is Parque Forestal, a popular promenade where you will find the imposing Museum of Fine Arts (Museo de Bellas Artes). Continuing east for a further five blocks, you will arrive at Plaza Italia.

Cross over the smelly Mapocho river and you reach Bellavista, the bohemian area of Santiago, with its many restaurants, galleries, theatres and a street market on Friday and Saturday evenings in Calle Andres Bello. Calle Purismo boasts many good restaurants; try La Tasca for excellent Spanish food, El Caramaño for typical Chilean fare and La Divina Comida for authentic Italian. Pablo Neruda, the Nobel Prize winner for Literature, lived in Bellavista, and his house, 'La Chascona' is open to the public.

Bordering Bellavista is Parque Metropolitano and Cerro San

Cristóbal from which, however short your stay, you should try to watch the sunset. You can walk to the top of Cerro San Cristóbal or take the funicular. Behind you the Andes with their 6000 metre snow-capped peaks will, smog and rain permitting, be in full view — a magnificent sight. The peaks that will stand out most clearly are Cerros San Ramón and Provincia in the *precordillera* (see *Around Santiago*, page 71).

The best arts and crafts in Santiago can be found in the Los Dominicos market. It is open Tuesday to Sunday from 10.00am until around 8.00pm (in winter it closes a little earlier). Although the quality of items is excellent, it can be expensive. To get there, take a Los Dominicos bus from Alameda in the direction of the *cordillera*.

The newspaper, *El Mercurio*, lists daily evening entertainment and events. Ballet, opera and classical music concerts are held in the classic Teatro Municipal (worth a visit if just for the interior).

Transport
In Santiago
Transport in Santiago hinges on the spotless and highly efficient **metro**, which with its connecting **bus** and **colectivo** (shared taxis running a fixed route) services can get you to all parts of the city cheaply and quickly. There are two main lines, one running east-west under the Alameda, and the other north-south.

Taxis are relatively cheap but do not expect them to know every street or expect the drivers to have a street directory.

Out of Santiago
If you intend to travel to other parts of Chile, tickets are best purchased at the main terminals. **Buses** to the south and to the coast leave from Alameda 3878, and those to the north from Terminal del Norte, intersection of Mackenna and Amunátegui. Competition between bus companies is fierce so prices are negotiable, particularly out of season (April to November).

Trains run from Santiago to Temuco all year round and in the summer the service is extended to Puerto Montt. Be warned — maintenance of the line is not the government's top priority!

There are three domestic **airlines**; Ladeco (Coronel Santiago Bueras 112, tel 39 5053); LanChile (Estado 10, tel 39 5053 and Saba Huérfanos 835, tel 632 5164). There are daily flights to all major cities. Ladeco and LanChile offer a special package for foreigners.

Shops and communications

In Santiago, **shops** are open Monday to Friday from 10.00am to 8.00pm and on Saturday from 10.00am to 2.00pm. Some shopping centres in the residential districts are open on Sundays. But some shops, particularly outside the cities, are prone to close at lunch time.

In the coastal cities of Iquique in the north and Punta Arenas in the south you can purchase duty free goods.

Banks open from 9.00am to 2.00pm, Monday to Friday. *Casas de Cambio* often stay open all day and some also open on Saturdays but their rates do not seem to be as good as the banks.

Post offices are open Monday to Friday from 8.30am to 6.00pm. The main post office in Santiago is at Agustinas 1137, Plaza de Armas.

Shops and banks are closed on the following **public holidays**: January 1, Easter, May 1, May 21, Corpus Christi (in May or June), June 29, August 15, September 18 and 19, October 12, November 1 and December 8 and 25.

Entel and CTC operate probably the most efficient **telephone** system in Latin America. International calls can be made direct from anywhere in the country, using either a public phone or one of the Entel or TC centres.

Maps

In common with most Latin American countries, Chile has an Instituto Geográfico Militar, a rather more military version of the USGS or the British Ordnance Survey. They do not extend the maps beyond the Argentine border, so you find that some maps are largely blank, which is useful if you run out of loo paper, but not if you are planning an international hike! You will find their sales office in Santiago city centre on the corner of Moneda and San Antonio, or at Av. Libertador Bernard O'Higgins 240, shop 3. Their 1:50,000 series is excellent and well worth investing in, especially if you are going to the Lakes District. (The sheets needed are given under each hike.) All the Institute's maps are subsidized, and prices are pretty reasonable. If you want to buy maps before you go, Stanfords bookshop in London sells some IGM maps.

What to buy

As in other Latin American countries, the best buys in Chile are Indian products: clothing, rugs, jewellery and basketwork. These are cheapest in the areas where they are made. Try the markets in

Temuco, Chillán and Puerto Montt. In Santiago and in main provincial cities you can buy good quality stuff at Cema-Chile shops (Av. Portugal 351, Santiago). Then, of course, there is Chilean wine.

National parks

Chile claims to have 50 national parks, but these are not all national parks in the internationally accepted sense. Great progress has been made, however, in achieving a balance between conservation and tourism, and all the parks are now administered with this balance uppermost in mind.

The hikes in this book will take you to a number of national parks, the largest being Torres del Paine in Patagonia. If you would like to know more about the ones we have not mentioned, write to the Corporación Nacional Forestal (CONAF). See *Addresses* at the end of the chapter.

Rescue Service

Cuerpo Socorro Andino is a voluntary service with which walkers may leave details of their expeditions in case of accident or failure to return. They will ask you for details of those in your party (name, addresses and ages), a contact number in Santiago, colour of tents, backpacks and jackets (for identification by helicopter), return date and planned route. There is no charge for registering, nor if you are rescued. In return, all they ask you to do is notify them immediately upon your return. See *Addresses*, next page.

Camping supplies

There are a number of stores in Santiago where you can buy, sell or rent new and used camping equipment.

Southern Summits have a very good range of equipment for sale. Whilst the imported equipment is very expensive, some of the locally manufactured clothing is quite reasonable. They also rent everything from boots to ropes to tents, but advance reservations are recommended. They organize expeditions or can provide a guide, if required. Highly recommended. 102-104 Merced, tel 39 3712 or fax 33 7784, hours 10.00am to 8.00pm.

There is a small store (no name) in the same building as the Federacíon Andinismo, Alduante Simpson 77, Metro Baquedano. It has a good range of new equipment, but is quite expensive. No equipment rented.

Luz Sanhueza Quiroz runs a small store that stocks good quality camping and climbing equipment. She is occasionally able to rent equipment and will consider purchasing used equipment. Portal Lyon, Shop 14 on the corner of Av. Providencia and Av. Los Leones, Metro Los Leones. Open Monday to Friday 10.30am to 1.00pm, 3.00pm to 8.00pm and on Saturday 10.30am to 2.00pm.

Reinaldo Lippi manufactures excellent clothes and backpacks either off the rack or made to measure. Toesca 2171, Metro Republica, tel 689 0096. Open Monday to Friday 10.00am to 7.30pm

Chinese Proveedores, Merced 525, imports a wide variety of Chinese foodstuffs, including easily prepared lightweight noodle-based meals. Be warned, the spicy ones will knock the socks off a spicy vindaloo.

ADDRESSES

The National Tourist Board (Sernatur), Av. Providencia 1550, tel 696 0474. Open Monday to Friday 9.00am to 6.30pm. There is also an office at the airport and offices in most major cities. The best guide book on Chile is the two-volume *Turistel*, which has excellent maps and lots of information.

Instituto Geográfico Militar, Corner of Moneda and San Antonio in the city centre or Av. Libertador Bernard O'Higgins 240, Shop 3.

Cuerpo Socorro Andino, Ricardo Cumming 329, tel 136 (often not answered) or 699 4764. Also at Southern Summits, Merced 102-104.

River rafting. For trips down the Maipo or Bío Bío rivers, try Altue Expediciones, Encomenderos 83, tel 232 1103 (English spoken), Access Adventure Travel, Huérferanos 786, tel 38 4938 or Expediciones Grado Diez (recommended), Las Urbinas 56, tel 251 2804.

Photography. Maurizio Moretto, Merced 753, Shop 2. Excellent service and high quality reproductions. For black and white try Foto Blanco y Negro, Estado 257, Shop 18. Professional and very reasonable. They also sell very cheap but high quality black and white film.

Corporación Nacional Forestal (CONAF), General Bulnes 259 (tel 696 0783). Ask for the Departamento de Conservación del Medio Ambiente (Conservation of the Environment Department).

Federación de Andinismo de Chile, Almirante Simpson 77, Santiago (tel 222 0888). Open 11.30am to 1.30pm, 3.30pm to 7.00pm Monday to Friday.

Asociación de Centros de Ski de Chile, Roger de Flor 2911, Santiago (tel 231 3411).

Accommodation Casa Paxi is a friendly hostel for climbers and hikers run by Pieter Jan van Bunningen (from Holland). Advice, maps, English spoken.

A highly recommended *hospedaje* is the family home of Ivonne and Albert Peirano. They are friendly, helpful and provide excellent food. Their address is Malaga 529, Depto 301, Las Condes, Santiago (tel 228 5074 or 850 1473).

Ships and ferries. For details of ships from Puerto Montt to Puerto Natales, try Naviera Magallanes (Navimag), Av. Suiza 248, Cerrillos, Santiago (tel 253318, telex 240069). Or book through Turismo Cocha, Agustinas 1173 (tel 698 3341). Navimag also have offices in Puerto Montt at Terminal Transbordadores, Angelmó (tel 2754 or 3318); and in Punta Arenas at Independencia 830 (tel 22593). In Puerto Natales they have an office at the port.

For trips to Puerto Aisén, Laguna San Rafael or Chacabuco, try Transcontainer/Empremar: Estado 360, Oficina 502c, Santiago (tel 337 118); or Av. Diego Portales 1450, Puerto Montt (tel 2548).

English bookshops: Eurotex, Providencia 2653, Loc.10 (tel 232 6035); Librería Inglesa, Pedro de Valdivia 47 (tel 231 9970).

Vegetarian restaurants: El Huerto, Orrego Luco 54, Providencia (tel 231 9889); El Naturalista, Moneda 846 (tel 698 4122); El Vegetariano, Huérfanos 827, Loc.18 (tel 397063).

British Embassy and Consulate, La Concepción 177, 4th floor, Providencia 1800, Casilla 72-D.

US Embassy, Agustinas 1343.

Australian Embassy, Gertrudis Echeñique 420, Las Condes.

Argentine Embassy, Vicuña Mackenna 41.

GERIATREKS

By Janet Cross

We have always been keen walkers, and our daughter, some years ago, sent a postcard from Puerto Montt saying: "Listen you two, you'd better get out here before you kick it." As our 80th birthdays approached we thought we should take up the suggestion while we were still mobile. At our age we did not want to travel with a group, but we needed the trip to be tailor-made to our requirements, which were lots of beautiful scenery with opportunities for walking, and comfortable transport and accommodation. This was achieved by Supersonic Travel of 13, Villiers St, London, who arranged everything including knowledgeable driver/guides where necessary.

We went in November, flying to Santiago via Rio de Janeiro, and from there took the train south to Puerto Varas. The journey lasted 22 hours and was a bit of an ordeal because of the jolting of the train and lack of sleeping car (we had reclining chairs). But it only cost £10 and the scenery was most beautiful, as green as Ireland, with many rivers and rich agricultural land. We took our first proper walk by Lake Llanquihue with its magnificent snow-covered volcano, Osorno, the far side. Next day we continued by bus to Puerto Montt.

We flew to Punta Arenas where we were met by our guide and his car. Roberto took us to Torres del Paine National Park where we spent three perfect days staying in the very comfortable hotel at Pehoé, and taking daily walks. Roberto drove us to different parts of the park each day and his knowledge of the locality and the flora and fauna added much to our enjoyment. We will always remember the peace and beauty of that park — one of the loveliest places we have ever been.

The next journey was into Argentina, driving with Roberto via a little-used border post. Crossing the Patagonian desert is so boring it is almost fascinating. Not sand, but coarse grass, but of such poverty it only supports 1-2 sheep per square kilometre. In Calafate we went to the Perito Moreno glacier — every bit as impressive as we had been led to believe — then on to Rio Gallegos from where we visited a penguin colony. There were a great number of birds nesting among dwarf juniper bushes and I am all in favour of the arrangements — the female lays the eggs and then hands over responsibility to the male who does the sitting.

Bariloche was our final destination before flying to Buenos Aires and home. We arrived on Brian's 80th birthday and found a cake, champagne and red roses waiting in our hotel room. We enjoyed some wonderful walking here, much helped by chair lifts, which, although a little difficult for the wrinklies, enabled us to reach the top of the mountains with rewarding views.

We both agreed that it was one of the best holidays we have ever had. The variety and beauty of the scenery, helpful guides, friendly people, comfortable hotels and absence of any tummy-troubles, made it just about perfect. If we could have persuaded the Argentines to eat dinner before 10 o'clock, it *would* have been perfect!

ARGENTINA FACTBOX

Area: 2,807,560 square kilometres

Length: 3460 kilometres

Average width: 750 kilometres

Coastline: 2575 kilometres

Population: 32.6 million

Mean monthly temperatures

Buenos Aires: 11°C (July) to 24°C (January)
Bariloche: 3°C (July) to 15°C (January)
Ushuaia: 2°C (July) to 10°C (January)

Public holidays

1st January   New Year's Day
6th January   Epiphany
25th February   San Martín's birthday
Holy Thursday
Good Friday
1st May   Labour Day
25th May   Independence Day
20th June   National Flag Day
9th July   Declaration of Independence
17th August   Anniversary of San Martin's death
8th December   Immaculate Conception
25th December   Christmas Day

Chapter Five

Argentina: essential facts

Introduction

Argentina, the second largest country in Latin America after Brazil, is a nation of contrasts and contradictions. Walk along the fashionable Calle Florida in Buenos Aires and you could be in Paris. Fly a couple of hours south to the barren pampas which make up most of the country's landscape and you could be in the Wild West. Argentina is an enigma also in terms of its economic development: although one of the richest countries in Latin America for natural resources, its economic problems have brought unprecedented poverty to a traditionally prosperous people.

From a walker's point of view Argentina offers almost inexhaustible possibilities. Broadly speaking the country can be divided into four main physical areas:

1. The Andes, high and parched in the northwest on the border with Bolivia, glaciated in the Patagonian south where the mountain range finally plunges into the sea. The oases strung along the eastern foot of the Andes — Jujuy, Salta, Tucumán, Mendoza — were the first places to be colonized by the Spaniards and retain much of the architecture.
2. The North and Mesopotamia containing the vast plains of the Chaco and the floodplain between the Paraná and Uruguay rivers.
3. The Pampas lying south of the Chaco, east of the Andes and north of the Río Colorado. These cover some 650,000 square kilometres.
4. Patagonia, an area of windswept plateaux south of the Río Colorado which rise up into the snow-capped peaks of the Andes. This covers around 780,000 square kilometres.

Visas

British, American, Canadian, French and German citizens no longer need tourist visas for Argentina. Citzens of these countries will be given a 90-day visa on arrival. Australian and New Zealand passport holders will need to apply before arriving in Argentina. Along with their passport they will need to have completed the appropriate application form, supplied a 'letter of introduction from their bank' evidence of a return ticket and $30.

BUENOS AIRES

Introduction

More than any other capital city in Latin America, Buenos Aires ('BA' to its friends) dominates the country culturally, economically and psychologically. It is home to one third of the population, and this is where everything happens, which may endear it to you or it may not. With Rio de Janeiro it is easily the most cosmopolitan city on the continent, with Italian, Spanish, Portuguese, German and British communities and a large shifting population of more temporary visitors. The British community is perhaps the most interesting: they built Argentina's railways in the latter half of the 19th century, introduced wire fencing from the UK thus making cattle ranching big business, and have somehow managed to give the Spanish language an Oxford accent. Most stayed put during the Falklands War.

People born in Buenos Aires are called *Porteños* and their culture historically centres on the Boca, a maze of narrow streets clustered around the old port. This strange mixture of working people's homes and cafes, gentrified town houses and 'ethnic' tourist joints is still worth seeing, but do it quickly before the last of its original inhabitants sell out.

Things to do

Where in Buenos Aires is a free monthly guide, in English, with listings of what is happening, where to stay and where to shop in Buenos Aires.

Transport

Like Santiago, Buenos Aires has an efficient **metro** system known locally as the *Subte*.

Taxis are recognizable by their distinctive yellow and black colours. Drivers and their meters are not always reliable but fares should work out at about $1.50 per kilometre and approximately $45 for a fare to Ezeiza airport.

Bus to Eizeiza airport leaves from outside Hotel Gran Colón in Pellegrini 509. Journey takes approximately one hour.

Beyond Buenos Aires

There are seven domestic **airlines** Aerolíneas Argentinas (Calle Perú 2, tel 343 8551); LADE (Calle Perú 710, tel 361 7071); Austral Corrientes 485, tel 313 3777) Lapa, Cata, Transporte Aéreo Neugén (TAN) and LAER. There are daily flights to all major cities. Aerolíneas Argentinas offers tourists a special airpass fare for domestic travel.

For **hovercraft** or **ferry** services to Uruguay, try Aliscafos Belt, Av. Córdoba 787 (tel 382 4691) or Ferry Líneas (Florida 780, tel 392 4691).

Trains are somewhat unrealiable. In March 1993, the Argentine government withdrew funding for the railways, and since then many services have been suspended as the provinces do not have the resources to maintain them. Consequently, times are changing daily and becoming less and less reliable. For further information on transport, see *Travelling and Living*, page 22.

The long-distance **bus** terminal is adjacent to the Retiro rail station, a short walk from the subway (Línea C). All long-distance bus services must operate from this terminal.

For information on trains there is an information centre beside Galerías Pacífico at Florida 729, tel 311 6411. Trains depart from different stations depending on their destination. Read Paul Theroux's book the *Old Patagonian Express* before you depart, or better still take it to read en route.

Shops and communications

In Buenos Aires, **shops** usually open at 9.00am and stay open in many cases until 7.00pm Monday to Friday. On Saturdays they are generally open only in the morning. Outside Buenos Aires, shops will often close for a mid-day siesta.

Bureau de Changes or *Casas de Cambio* are generally open from 8.30am to 4.30pm, Monday to Friday and some operate on Saturday mornings. **Banks** tend to have shorter hours, weekdays only, closing around 3.00pm. Most are found on Corrientes or San Martin.

The **central post office** or *correo central* is at the corner of Sarmiento and LN Alem and open Monday to Friday from 8.00am to 8.00pm and Saturday 8.00am to 2.00pm.

There is an Entel **(telephone)** office at Corrientes 707 which opens 24 hours every day of the week. They also have offices throughout the country.

Banks, government offices and most shops close for the following **public holidays**: January 1; April 17, May 1, May 25, June 10, June 20, July 9, August 17, October 12, December 25.

Maps

The Argentine map-making agency is the Instituto Geográfico Militar. There is a small sales office at Cabildo 301 (Subte D to Ministero Carranza or take bus 152 from Retiro) open Monday to Friday 8.00am to 1.00pm. The Institute's 1:500,000 series is a work of art, and Sheets 3972 (Junín de los Andes) and 4172 (San Carlos de Bariloche) are musts for anyone going to the Lakes District. Unfortunately their scale is too small to be of much use on the hikes, but they make good souvenirs. The 1:100,000 series is better on detail, but the sheets we looked at were very out of date and omitted some of the trails. Not worth bothering about unless the ones you want have been revised. The Institute's prices are heavily subsidized and very good value for money.

A series of maps for trekkers and mountaineers is published by Ediciones Dhaulagiri. Mostly scale 1:250,000, these are available mail-order. Write to Eduardo Magnani, Av. José V. Zapata 48- 50 B (5500) Mendoza (if you are in the area phone 242476) for a list and current prices.

In the national parks, the *guardaparques* (park rangers) keep excellent maps in their posts around the parks. You can get overall maps of the parks at the office of the Servicio Nacional de Parques Nacionales. It is often difficult to buy them at the national parks themselves. In Bariloche, the Club Andino Bariloche at Calle 20 de Febrero 30 has excellent maps of the Lakes District in its library. If you want to buy maps before you go, try Stanfords bookshop in London which sells some IGM maps, plus the South American Explorers Club map of Aconcagua.

What to buy

Some of the best leather goods in the world can be bought in Argentina, from leather jackets, shoes, horse saddles to leather *bombachas*, the baggy trousers worn by gauchos. Equally fascinating are the gourds which all self-respecting Argentine males keep by them for drinking *yerba mate*. Something of a national addiction, this concoction is imbibed communally through a silver tube called a *bombilla*. Very good for ensuring conviviality, curing colds and making you feel sick. The gourd and *bombilla* are guaranteed to remind you of all these things as they sit on your mantelpiece in future years. In Bariloche, you can buy good sweaters, jams and chocolates, while in Salta you will find beautiful ponchos and pottery. Then, of course, there is Argentine wine.

National parks
Argentina's national parks are fewer in number than Chile's, but just as well organized. Nahuel Huapí National Park, the first in South America, was established in 1903, and Argentina continues to lead the field, with 12 parks run on similar lines to those in the United States. Tourism is actively encouraged, all parks permit camping and many have hotels or hostels to accommodate the numerous visitors. The influx of Argentine tourists, however, tends to be restricted to the summer months of January and February and it is not difficult to find solitude if you want it.

Apart from Nahuel Huapí, the other national parks covered by the walks in this book include Los Glaciares National Park in Patagonia, Tierra del Fuego National Park and Los Alerces National Park in Chubut province.

Trekking and expedition organizations
Several companies have opened which specialize in organized trekking or expedition logistics. This is an option well worth considering if you are an inexperienced backpacker but are longing to see the southern Andes, or if you are mounting an expedition and need local assistance.

Trekking S.A., Paraguay 542 2° "C" (1057) Buenos Aires (tel 312 6853).
Treks include Aconcagua and Fitz Roy, along with several horseback trips.

Caminante, Deloqui 368, 9410 Ushuaia, Tierra del Fuego (tel 0901 22723).
The only agency in Tierra del Fuego that specializes in adventure travel, they provide a variety of activities: trekking, canoeing, horseriding, cross-country skiing, and have been recommended for their environmental sensitivity.

Ediciones Dhaulagiri — Expedition Department, Av. José V. Zapata 48 - 50 B (5500) Mendoza (tel 242476).
They promote themselves as expedition organizers who can

provide information, maps and a library of expedition reports, etc. They will arrange transport, mules, permits... everything. The area covered is between Puna and the southern Patagonian icecap.

Jorge Tarditti, C.P. 9405 El Chalten (tel 0966 20408 6/15). Experienced mountaineer and trekking guide for Fitz Roy area. Can provide equipment, transport, etc.

ADDRESSES

National Tourist Office (*Casa de Turismo*) Suipacha 1111 (tel 312 5611 or 312 5621). Tourist office organizes tours of Buenos Aires. There are also information kiosks at either end of Calle Florida. In addition, there are *Casas de Turismo* for each region.

National Parks Information Service (Servicio Nacional de Parques Nacionales), Santa Fe 680, Buenos Aires.

Argentine Wildlife Foundation (Fundacíon Vida Silvestre Argentina), Defensa 245/251, Buenos Aires. This conservation organization and bookshop has information and books on Argentine flora and fauna.

Club Andinista Mendoza, Calles Pardo and Ruben Lemos, Mendoza.

Club Andino Bariloche, 20 de Febrero 30, Bariloche.

British Embassy Luis Agote 2412/52 (tel 803 7070).

US Embassy Cervino 4320 (tel 774 6841).

Australian Embassy, Av. Santa Fe 846 (Swissair building) (tel 312 6841).

Part Two:

Regional Guide to the Walks

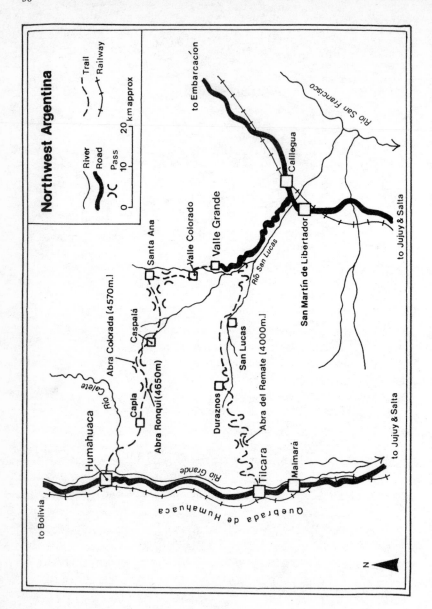

Northwest Argentina

River
Road
Pass
Trail
Railway

0   10   20 km approx

to Embarcación

Río San Francisco

Callegua

Santa Ana

Valle Colorado

Valle Grande

Abra Colorada (4570 m.)

Caspalá

Río San Lucas

Abra Ronquí (4650 m)

San Martín de Libertador

to Jujuy & Salta

Capla

San Lucas

Durazno

Abra del Remate (4000 m.)

Río Cajete

Humahuaca

Abra del Remate (4000 m.)

Tilcara

Malimará

Río Grande

Quebrada de Humahuaca

to Bolivia

to Jujuy & Salta

N

Chapter Five

Northwest Argentina

by David Greenman, updated by Doris Stettler and others

Introduction

The mountainous province of Jujuy (pronounced 'hoo-huey'), 100 kilometres south of the Bolivia/ Argentina border, is one of the most primitive backpacking areas in Argentina. Its friendly hardworking people and the terrain are very similar to those of Peru, Bolivia and other Andean countries. The inhabitants depend on sheep for a living and survive on a humble diet of potatoes and corn. They will be more than glad to tell you which way to go when you come to a fork in the trail.

Many of the paths were made by local Indians when the Incas plundered their tribal fortresses or *pucarás*, the ruins of which can still seen in the Quebrada de Humahuaca to the west. Well worn paths branch off each trail, often leading to small *ranchos*, so you may have to backtrack occasionally to stay on the main track.

The two hikes in this region are different from the others described in this book in that they are better done in winter (May to October) rather than summer. This is because winter here is the dry season. Although nights can be very cold, with occasional snow on the high passes, the temperature rises into the seventies (fahrenheit) during the day, so be prepared for all types of weather.

In many ways this part of the Andes resembles the desert of the southwest United States. To start with there are small thorny trees and shrubs, then as you go above the treeline there is just stubby grass. As you approach the Quebrada de Humahuaca this is replaced by different types of cactus. Local people are very knowledgeable about the different types of herbs used for medication, such as *rica rica*, a dry shrub with a delicious flavour for tea that calms the stomach. At higher altitudes, there is a plant whose small leaves, if crushed between the fingers and inhaled, will cure headaches and nausea caused by the altitude. There are many others, but enquire locally before experimenting with your own brew.

Wildlife is also abundant here and you may well spot a family of condors riding the air currents in search of carrion. Other animals include the vicuña and the viscacha, a larger version of the chinchilla which lives near the highest passes and makes a shrill whistle as it jumps from rock to rock.

If you show respect, the people of this area will be very friendly in return. When a *campesino* goes by leading his pack train, step aside and stop. He will also stop and exchange words for a few minutes, and a wealth of local knowledge may be reaped. Treat local villagers as your hosts. Remember that you are walking on their trail, which they use regularly and maintain themselves.

Getting there

By air and bus Take an Aerolíneas Argentinas flight from Buenos Aires to either Salta or Jujuy. Flights to both take two hours. From Salta, take an Atahualpa bus to San Martín de Libertador, commonly referred to as San Martín (two and a half hours). From Jujuy take a Balut bus to San Martín de Libertador (an hour and a half). Or you can take a bus to Tilcara (one and a half hours) or Humahuaca (three and a half hours).

By train and bus Take a train from Retiro station in Buenos Aires to Tucumán (11 trains a week, journey takes around 24 hours). In Tucumán, take a bus to Salta (four to five hours), then an Atahualpa bus to San Martín. If planning to get to Salta from Buenos Aires via Tucumán, buy your train ticket to Tucumán and your bus ticket to Salta at the same time so you can transfer directly to the bus which meets the train. This way you avoid having to go to the local bus terminal and waiting.

San Martín de Libertador is probably the best place to start the hikes (see map), but they may also be started in the Quebrada de Humahuaca which is equally accessible by public transport.

VALLE GRANDE TO HUMAHUACA

Directions

NOTE: If you decide to start from Humahuaca towards Valle Grande, walk southeast out of the town towards the Río Calete. The trail from the Calete valley to Caspala is difficult to find, but local residents will point out the way. However, as we started at Valle Grande, we give directions from there.

Use the diagram on page 64 to plan camp sites. Normal sources of water are also shown.

There is no public transport to Valle Grande from San Martín de Libertador and it is a strenuous 93 kilometre walk. If you do not feel like walking, you will have to hitch with the logging trucks which ply the road but be prepared to be patient as they do not go every day. Doris Stettler reports that the shopkeeper from Valle Grande, Señor Arjona, drives to Valle Grande twice a week and will take passengers for a fee of about $15. Enquire at the *guardaparque*, eight kilometres from Libertador. The route is breathtaking as it skirts canyons that seem bottomless. This sub-tropical area is a national park so if you are observant, you may spot monkeys and toucans.

In Valle Grande you can buy last minute provisions or a wide-brimmed hat handmade from local wool. The trail leaves from the north of Valle Grande and follows the valley up to Valle Colorado, another small village. There are very few good camping spots or water sources between here and Santa Ana, the next village, so you might prefer to spend the night in Valle Colorado and fill your canteen early next morning. From Valle Colorado it is a strenuous seven hour climb to the high pass from where you enjoy splendid views of the canyons. At the top of the pass, look out for a cross on your left. Turn off left here and walk down into the Santa Ana valley.

Santa Ana is a quaint, sleepy *adobe* village 3660 metres above sea level, with one main street. Many people have moved down to the lowlands for better jobs, but 100 or so still remain to care for the family sheep. There used to be a small copper mine here, but it went out of business many years ago because of the lack of transport. You can still see the remains southwest of the village. Santa Ana is a good place to stop as there are many places near the river to camp, and the communal water supply is nearby. You can buy the very bare essentials at the small general store but the store in Caspalá is much better equipped.

From Santa Ana take the path that climbs the hill to the right of the canyon. The path then divides. Ignore the path which branches off right around the hilltops. Instead, follow the path which leads down into the valley ahead and then climbs up to a second pass. From here you catch your first glimpse of Caspalá, another picturesque village nestling in the deep valley below. All you see initially is a small white church as the surrounding houses blend in perfectly with the mountainside. About 10 kilometres before Caspalá you descend a steep, seemingly endless, slope called Las Lajutas. At the bottom is a fast flowing stream, ideal for refreshing hot, tired feet. The path then climbs for about one and a half hours before reaching Caspalá. In Caspalá, ask permission to pitch camp in someone's yard or pasture. Every flat space is put to some use: a home, crops, or livestock. Santa Ana to Caspalá takes about six hours.

The final stretch of the journey is a long one (two days), with very few signs of human life between Caspalá and Humahuaca. Rob and Jo Withers suggest taking three days, rather than the two described here. The best place to spend the night is at Abra Colorada at 4570 metres. This is actually the nicest camping spot on the entire hike, with plenty of short grass to pitch a tent on and springs to drink from. It is also a good place to see viscachas and vicuñas. It is about two hours before the pass, Abra Ronqui.

Abra Colorada is the last place you are certain to find water until Río Calete, so stock up — it is a long and dry walk.

After Abra Colorada the path climbs to Abra Ronqui, the highest point at 4650 metres, and then descends steeply into Capla (allow two and a half hours). In Capla the path leaves the road to the right. After 10 minutes, the path forks, and you take the right branch. Río Calete is almost two hours walk. Doris Stettler reports that it is difficult to find the trail on the other side of the river. She suggests crossing the river and following the bank downstream until you find a pile of stones from where the path leaves the river and starts climbing again. It will take a little over two hours to reach Humahuaca from Río Calete.

Humahuaca, at 2940 metres, is a small traditional town of several thousand inhabitants. It stands in the stunning Quebrada de Humahuaca with its dramatic rocks and giant cacti. Allow yourself at least two days to relax and take in the sights, before continuing through Argentina or proceeding to Bolivia.

VALLE GRANDE TO TILCARA

This hike is a bit more rigorous than the one above as it has many steep ascents and descents. A third of it is below the treeline which makes it easy to find shade. We did it in summer, but will wait until winter next time since we were almost overcome by heat exhaustion. In contrast to the hike further north, there are no communities in this area in which to seek first aid.

Directions

NOTE: If you do this hike the other way round you can get buses and trains from Jujuy in the direction of Quebrada de Humahuaca. Get out at Tilcara and, on the south side of the town, follow the sign to the Garganta del Diablo, a deep gorge from which the town receives its water supply. Just past the waterworks leave the road on a track branching to the right. This soon splits. Take the uphill trail to the left. It is fairly clear from now on (follow the mule droppings) leading past Casa Blanca and up over the Abra del Remate towards Libertador.

If you start from the road leading from San Martín de Libertador to Valle Grande, ask to get off where the trail to San Lucas and Tilcara branches off. (It can be seen across the canyon to the southwest). If you manage the steep dusty ascent up the numerous switchbacks you will survive the rest of the hike. Near the end of the five-kilometre climb, you reach an abandoned hut to the right of the trail. This is an excellent place to rest, but the spring, hidden in the trees about 200 paces south, is a bit difficult to find.

After about 13 kilometres you reach San Lucas, which consists of a string of scattered houses. There are plenty of good grassy camping spots. But if you are camping near someone's *rancho*, be sure to meet the family with some sign of friendship: they may not realize your good intentions.

After another 26 kilometres of hiking you will reach Duraznos, a few buildings including a small school hugging the side of the mountain. From Duraznos it is a two-day walk to the 4000-metre pass called Abra del Remate. It is then three hours (14km) downhill to Tilcara, a pretty village in the Quebrada de Humahuaca with a handful of hotels and museums. From here you can visit a *pucará* (tribal fortress). For a place to stay in Tilcara, El Antigal is recommended. The elderly owner is very kind and helpful.

Practical information

Distance/time:

Valle Grande to Humahuaca

San Martín de Libertador to Valle Grande: 93 kilometres (no public transport. In the summer months or wet season the road is in a terrible state and few vehicles use it).

Valle Grande to Valle Colorado: nine kilometres (three hours).

Valle Colorado to Santa Ana: 16 kilometres (five to six hours).

Santa Ana to Caspalá: 20 kilometres (seven to eight hours).

Caspalá to Abra Colorada: 20 kilometres (seven hours).

Abra Colorada to Humahuaca: 30 kilometres (ten hours).

VALLE GRANDE TO TILCARA
Valle Grande road to San Lucas: 20 kilometres (ten hours).
San Lucas to Duraznos: 26 kilometres (11/12 hours).
Duraznos to Abra del Remate: 35 kilometres (15 hours or two days).
Abra del Remate to Tilcara: seven kilometres (two hours, all downhill).

Preparations: Wood for cooking is practically non-existent along much of the way, so a stove is recommended. The mountain people use shrubs and grass for fuel, but these are not plentiful so they appreciate visitors who leave this natural fuel for their own use. Kerosene is available locally, and gasoline/petrol (*nafla*) can sometimes be bought in larger towns or in Jujuy and Salta.

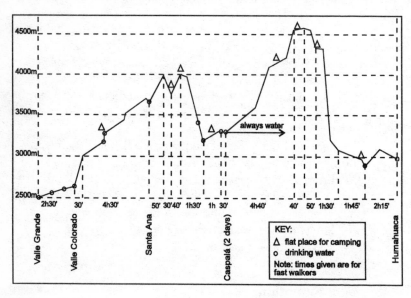

Chapter Six

Aconcagua

Introduction

With its summit of 6960 metres (22,840 feet), Aconcagua, just inside Argentina, is the highest mountain in the Americas. Its claim to be the king of the mountains, however, has not been without dispute. Traditionally the mountain had always been quoted as 7021 metres but a Chilean expedition to a remote part of the Andes, east of Copiapó, reported that they had found a mountain called Ojos del Salado (shared with Chile) to be 7087 metres. Feverish activity followed,  including further surveying expeditions to both mountains and heated correspondence in the mountaineering press. The most recent (Italian-Argentine) expedition in 1989 came out with the following verdict: Aconcagua, 6960 metres (22,840 feet); Ojos del Salado, 6887 metres (22,638 feet).

The first recorded climb of Aconcagua was by Matias Zurbriggen of the Fitzgerald Expedition in January 1897. But there is evidence that Araucanian and Aymara Indians peopled the sides of the mountain hundreds of years ago, later to be invaded by the Incas from Peru. The Incas called the grand peak Ancocahua, which means 'white sentinel' in Quechua. In 1985 an Inca mummy, complete with colourful poncho, was found just below the summit. From this find and others, archaeologists believe that the Inca chiefs offered their children as sacrifice to the Inca god.

The summit can be approached from the south, west or east faces, depending on your mountaineering expertise, but the 'normal' route is up the west side. However, although this route is not technically difficult, Aconcagua's treacherous weather conditions make it an extremely challenging ascent that should be attempted only by fit, acclimatized and experienced climbers. Apart from the effects of

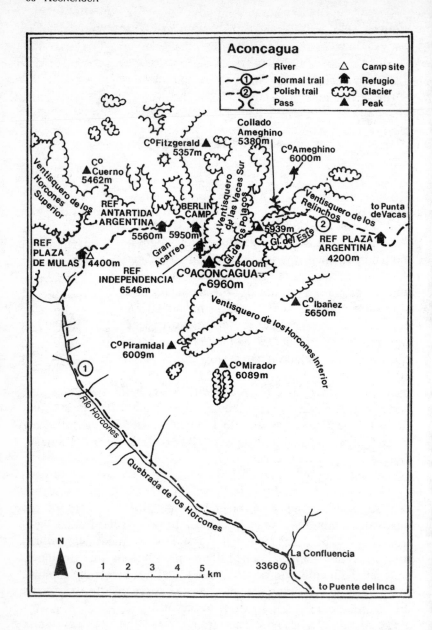

altitude, you are likely to battle against winds of up to 240 kilometres an hour and temperatures that plummet to minus 30°C. During the past 60 years nearly 100 people have died on Aconcagua and every year climbers lose fingers and toes through frostbite.

The second most common ascent is the Polish route from the east which passes up the left edge of the Glaciar de los Polacos. Enquire at the Club Andinista Mendoza for details.

Aconcagua offers backpackers some good hiking around the base camp area (Refugio Plaza de Mulas).

Getting there

The climb starts at Puente del Inca, a 160-kilometre bus ride from the Argentine city of Mendoza. The local bus is cheapest, otherwise use the international bus. You can also get to Puente del Inca direct from Santiago. If catching an international bus, check with the driver that you will be allowed off at Puente del Inca before you board. It is also a good idea to ensure your baggage is easily accessible. Now that the Argentine government has completed a new border control about half a mile from Puente del Inca, you will find that the international buses will drop you off here unless you request otherwise.

The ascent

At Puente del Inca (2718 metres), which takes its name from the incredible natural bridge on which it stands, you can stay overnight at the Hostería Puente del Inca ($40 without meals) or there is space to camp, if you prefer. Patrick Frew reports that the restaurant by the Puente has bunk-bed accommodation for about $10 and a sort of climbing hut atmosphere. The owner also has detailed maps of Aconcagua and the area for sale.

Mules for carrying equipment to Base Camp can be rented here. However, there are reports that these are becoming extortionately expensive. Fernando Grajales and Eduardo Cruzatte are the best-known muleteers. *The South American Explorer* reported in early 1993 that:

... there is such a demand for mules during the peak climbing season that Grajales can maximize his revenues by having his mules take one party's stuff up to Mulas in one day, returning that same day to Puente with another party's stuff. He is no longer willing (without considerable negotiation) to have his mules accompany a party up to the half-way point at lower or upper Confluencia, spend the night there (which is good for the group's acclimatization) and proceed the

rest of the way up to Mulas the second day. Instead, he or his
assistant Andrea Garcia will insist on the mules taking your stuff all
the way while you spend the night at Grajales' camp at lower
Confluencia — sleeping in his tents, on his foam pads, buying a meal
from his cook tent, etc. This works equally well for your
climatization but not for your wallet. We declined to accept his
conditions, so we did not stay at his camp. We heard that this
coerced hospitality at the camp comes with a tab of $50 per person.

The same article mentions that the cheapest price they were able to
negotiate for the round trip was $150 per mule. Mules will carry up
to 60 kilograms. They also report that Grajales and his crew have
been 'assigned' by the ranger the prime camping spaces at Mulas for
the sole use of their clients.

It is recommended that climbers spend a few days acclimatizing
in Puente del Inca before setting out on the 37 kilometre walk to
Base Camp, a climb of 1700 metres. The hike can be done in ten
hours by acclimatized and fit people, but it is best to take two or
three days to help you adjust to the altitude, so you will need to
carry a tent. This is recommended anyway, as the dilapidated huts
are overcrowded in peak season.

Base Camp, for the standard route, is at Plaza de Mulas Superior
(4400 metres), at the head of the Horcones valley. A smart hotel has
been built here (Refugio Plaza de Mulas, $140 per person full
board) which has a helicopter service if you cannot face haggling
over the cost of mules! There is also a small hut which gets very
crowded in peak season. Fill up on clean water from the streams
above the camp; further up the water tends to be a chocolate colour,
although it is all right to drink when it has settled. Most people
spend a few days here going on day hikes to build up strength.
Some nice glaciated peaks can be done in about two days as training
climbs.

Further up there are good camping places but you will have to melt
snow for water. Incidentally, you should try to drink between three
and five litres a day to prevent getting dehydrated by the altitude.

The path, easily visible, ascends a steep scree slope in broad
switchbacks beside a large glacier. After six to seven hours you
reach the Refugio Antártida Argentina (5560 metres), also known as
Nido de Condores, just to the right of Cerro Manso. You can stop
here or you may prefer to continue to the squalid collection of huts
400 metres higher up, known as Berlin Camp. It is best to spend
one or two days here to acclimatize further. Plenty of good camping
spots.

With 'only' 1000 metres to the summit, it is tempting to make this the last camp. However, only exceptionally strong and well acclimatized climbers make the summit in one long day from here. Most would be advised to go as far as the Refugio Independencia (6546 metres), about six hours further up. This hut, allegedly the highest in the world, is partly damaged and lets through the wind, but lies at a convenient point from which to make the final bid for the summit. A reader suggests making the last camp 200 metres above Berlin Camp from where it is about five to seven hours climb to the summit.

It is best to start early for the top, although you should wait until daylight if it is windy because strong winds make the body lose heat. The route is straightforward but you will find the last 300 metres very tiring. You cross a huge, steep and unstable field of boulders called the Gran Acarreo, then enter the notorious 45-degree couloir called the Canaleta. Keep on the right side of the gully, on the snow if possible, as the scree in the middle is very loose and steep and will wear you out. Concentrate on your footing and breathing. Gain the saddle between the north and south summits and continue left to the north summit. Circle the summit block to the left and follow the trail to the top. Allow six to nine hours from Independencia to the summit, more if conditions are bad or if you are suffering from altitude sickness. You should get back to Base Camp along the way you came in two days.

Practical information
Distance/time   The time needed for the climb depends on many factors but most people reckon on between nine and 15 days.

Preparations   This is one of the few peaks in South America for which you need a permit. This previously was a bureaucratic nightmare, requiring you to provide amongst other things a recent electrocardiogram (ECG) - not something most backpackers would think of packing! Now we are told you need only to complete some forms and hand over a mere $80 to the Subsecretaría Nacional de Turismo in Mendoza (Calle San Martín). It's marvellous what a heap of cash will dispense with! Permits need to be shown at the park entrance (before Plaza de Mulas) and may need to be shown again when you arive at Plaza de Mulas. The *guardaparque* will not allow anyone to enter without a permit, nor will they issue you with one. It's a long way back to Mendoza from the park entrance!

Adequate clothing and climbing equipment is vital. Many people use ski sticks, which help give balance on the scree slopes and in the Canaleta. Crampons, ice axe and ropes are advisable, though not essential. Because of the intense cold generated by the high winds, no climber should attempt Aconcagua in single boots. Plastic double boots are best. Duvet (down-filled) trousers, in addition to a duvet anorak (down parka), are also strongly recommended. It is a good idea to bring a tent, although make sure it is strong enough to withstand high winds. You can probably get by without one at the two highest *refugios*, but be prepared for them to be full. You will usually find spare food left by others, so carrying sufficient fuel is more important than food. You should buy both food and fuel in Mendoza (none in Puente del Inca). Finding white gas (*bencina*) can be a problem. Take a large water bottle as you will need to keep drinking to prevent dehydration. It is also a good idea to take Diamox for altitude sickness, but come down immediately if you think you may be getting pulmonary oedema (see *Health* section). Best time to make the ascent is January or February. Go earlier if you want to avoid the tours.

Guides/Muleteers Fernando Grajales, Andesport, JF Moreno 898, 5500 Mendoza or at Hostería Puente del Inca
Los Gateados, Cementerio Andinista, Puente del Inca, Mendoza (tel 54-61-290410 or fax 380367)
Eduardo Enrique Esteban, (a park ranger at Aconcagua) Huera Pire Expediciones, Suarez 171, Maipu, Mendoza 5515 (tel 54-61-973393 or fax 972866)

Tour operator Ace Travel in Santiago offer a 12-day hike up Aconcagua. More details from Ace Travel, Av. L. Bdo O'Higgins 949, 16th Floor, Santiago. Tel: (2) 695 4838/696 0391. Fax: (56 2) 672 7483.

Maps The best source of maps and information is probably the one from Ediciones Dhaulagiri (see page 55). Otherwise try the Club Andinista Mendoza in Calle Pardo y Lemos, Mendoza (tel 241840) or the Federación Argentina de Montanismo y Afines, Jose P Varela 3948, Buenos Aires (tel 531559). Also try Fernando Grajales, J F Moreno 898, 5500 Mendoza; or Luis Alberto Parra, Guiraldes 246, Guaymallén, 5519 Mendoza (tel 242 003). The best map we found was one published by the American Alpine Club in 1987, obtainable from the South American Explorers Club (see advert on page 148).

Chapter Seven

Around Santiago and Viña del Mar

Introduction

If, after several days of the smog and bustle of Santiago, you are hungry for fresh air and tranquillity, a pleasant alternative to heading to the coast is to make for the mountains and valleys to the northeast or southeast. In an hour or two you can be winding along a clear rushing river up into the Andean foothills or dangling your feet in a soothing thermal pool.

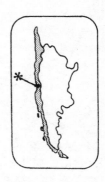

WALKS ON THE OUTSKIRTS OF THE CITY
by Nick Cotton

Camino del Cajón

Take the metro to Las Condes and then pick up a bus or *colectivo* to Arrayán and continue along the road into Sanctuario de la Naturaleza, otherwise known as the Camino del Cajón or Cajón del Arrayán. A small entrance fee must be paid at the park gates. The track is fairly straightforward. Follow the obvious path near the El Arrayán river past cacti and shrubs. You can bathe in the river, which although cold, is clean and invigorating after a few hours' walk. You can continue north for two or three days if you have time. Otherwise it makes a perfect day out with a picnic.

Cerro Manquehue

This mountain, shaped like a volcano with its cone knocked off, can be climbed in a few hours and, smog permitting, affords fabulous views of the city and the *cordillera* behind. Take a 108A or 45A bus from Escuela Militar metro station to the end of Américo Vespucio Norte and follow the obvious track up the hills west of the main peak and up on to the summit. Return the same way.

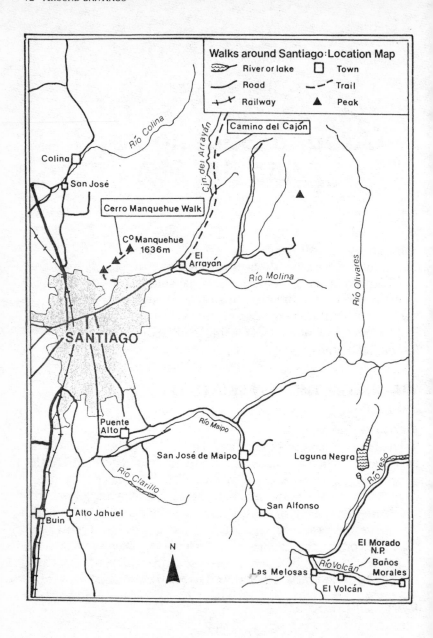

Walks around Santiago : Location Map

River or lake   Town
Road   Trail
Railway   Peak

Camino del Cajón

Cin. del Arrayán

Río Colina

Colina

San José

Cerro Manquehue Walk

Cº Manquehue
1636m

El Arrayán

Río Molina

Río Olivares

SANTIAGO

Puente Alto

Río Maipo

San José de Maipo

Laguna Negra

Río Yeso

Río Clarillo

Buin   Alto Jahuel

San Alfonso

N

El Morado
N.P.

Baños Morales

Las Melosas   Río Volcán

El Volcán

FURTHER AFIELD

Cajón de Maipo and El Morado National Park
by Christine and John Myerscough

The original Indian inhabitants of Chile walked through this and other valleys to cross the Andes into Argentina but because of the inhospitable terrain they never made permanent settlements. As a result, unlike in the Central Valley, the names of the attractive villages which dot the Maipo valley today are Spanish rather than Indian. Many are named after locally grown fruits, such as the peach and the almond, whose blossom is spectacular in spring. During Pinochet's years in power, these valleys were used as escape routes for dissidents fearful of his secret police.

You can reach San José de Maipo, 50 kilometres southeast of Santiago, in a little over one hour. Most day-trippers turn around and go back after reaching this colonial town, but it is well worth continuing to the end of the road to Baños Morales (thermal pools). A further two hours' walk takes you to the beautiful alpine meadows beside a small lake beneath the jagged pinnacles of the El Morado massif. With its peak of 4490 metres, the area is popular with Santiago climbers. However the highest peaks are for very experienced climbers and have only been climbed a few times. The small national park which occupies the valley below the peak is a refreshing spot to recover from nights out on the town in Santiago.

Getting there
Buses for the San José de Maipo leave every 15 minutes from Parque O'Higgins near the Metro of the same name. Only one bus a day goes all the way to Baños Morales, leaving at 7.30am arriving 11.00am, and returning to Parque O'Higgins from Baños Morales at 6.00pm. The one and a half hour journey up to San José de Maipo is pleasant, along paved roads all the way. En route you will pass large outdoor earth ovens and bars which serve traditional *empanadas* and are popular stopping-off points with day trippers. There are several camp sites, hostals and picnic stops on the way and San José has a large municipal camp site beside the river, with swimming pool and horse riding facilities.

Directions
After San José the road degenerates into a very dusty track. Small roadside stalls sell local delicacies such as walnuts and marzipan. If you had a late start, the beautiful town of San Alfonso is an

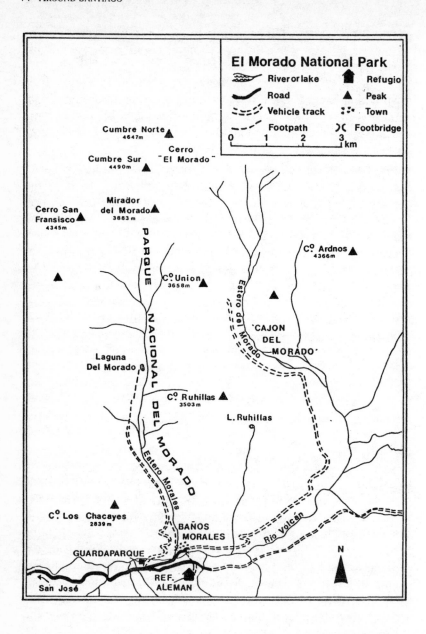

El Morado National Park

≈≈≈	River or lake		🏠	Refugio
▬	Road		▲	Peak
– – –	Vehicle track		፥	Town
– – –	Footpath		)(	Footbridge

0   1   2   3
                    km

Cumbre Norte ▲
4647m

Cerro
"El Morado"

Cumbre Sur ▲
4490m

Mirador
del Morado ▲
3883 m

Cerro San ▲
Fransisco
4345m

C° Ardnos ▲
4366m

PARQUE

C° Union ▲
3658m

▲

NACIONAL

'CAJON
DEL
MORADO'

Estero del Morado

DEL

Laguna
Del Morado

MORADO

C° Ruhillas ▲
3503 m

L. Ruhillas

Estero Morales

C° Los Chacayes ▲
2839 m

BAÑOS
MORALES

Rio Volcán

GUARDAPARQUE

N

San José

REF.
ALEMAN

excellent place to stop. It has plenty of *hosterías* and restaurants, as well as a camp site above the river, complete with barbeque pits and picnic tables. Nice views of the *cordillera*.

El Volcán, 22 kilometres on from San Alfonso, is a dusty little town with a bar and basic restaurant but no accommodation. From here it is about three hours' walk to Baños Morales. The route offers spectacular views up and down the Maipo canyon and passes a beautiful waterfall.

Shortly before reaching Baños Morales, about 12 kilometres after El Volcán, the road splits. Left goes to Baños Morales, while straight on is signposted Lo Valdes and leads past some mines, and on up the south side of the Río Volcán. Take the lefthand fork which soon splits again. This time, ignore the righthand road which leads to Baños Morales, and turn left and head down to the *guardería* just before the road crosses the river. This is the entrance to the El Morado National Park where you will be charged a small fee and given a ticket.

Continue up the road which soon steepens and starts to zigzag. About one kilometre from the park entrance you pass beneath a white cross from where you get the last views of the Maipo valley. One and a half hours from the park entrance, the road levels out and you get a superb view of the Mirador del Morado and behind it the mighty bulk of Cerro Morado (4490 metres). Another hour's walk brings you to the beautiful Laguna del Morado from where you can cross the moraines to the foot of the glaciers which descend the Morado massif.

Returning past the lake and beginning to retrace your steps down the valley, look out for some yellow/orange mineral deposits in the meadows to your left. These mark the site of many fresh water springs from which you can enjoy a refreshing cup of *agua mineral con gas* completely *gratis*. These meadows are ideal for camping.

It takes two to two and a half hours to get down to the small town of Baños Morales from the park. Retrace your steps as far as the top of the zigzags, but instead of following the road, take a small footpath leading left along the ridge. Soon you will look down on the steep sides valley of the Río Morales, and at its outlet into the main valley ahead, the first houses of Baños Morales. The path descends to cross the river by a small footpath at the edge of town. Here again you will find a small park kiosk and places to camp. Baños Morales has several *hosterías* and some popular thermal baths above the Río Volcán, which at this point flows through a deep gorge.

Eleven kilometres beyond Baños Morales the road ends at the

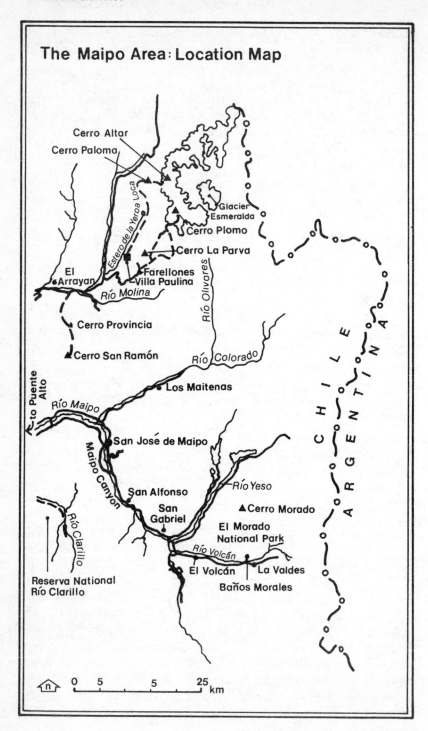

The Maipo Area: Location Map

Cerro Altar

Cerro Paloma

Glacier Esmeralda

Cerro Plomo

Cerro La Parva

Estero de la Yerva Loca

El Arrayan

Farellones
Villa Paulina

Río Molina

Río Olivares

Cerro Provincia

Cerro San Ramón

Río Colorado

to Puente Alto

Río Maipo

Los Maitenas

San José de Maipo

Maipo Canyon

San Alfonso

San Gabriel

Río Yeso

Cerro Morado

El Morado National Park

Río Volcán

El Volcán

La Valdes

Baños Morales

Río Clarillo

Reserva National Río Clarillo

CHILE

ARGENTINA

n 0 5   5   25 km

Baños de Colina, more natural thermal pools from where you can admire the snow-capped peaks while enjoying a hot swim. At the foot of the mountains is a lush valley from where you can do further sorties into the hills and lakes beyond (some do this on horseback).

If you have time, you should definitely visit the delightful Refugio Alemán at Lo Valdes, on the road to Termas de Colina not far after the turning to Baños Morales. This beautiful stone alpine chalet, set among verdant meadows and woods on the south side of the main valley, was founded by the German climbing club, but is open all year round to anyone and provides excellent food, drinks and accommodation. Around the hut can be found fossil remains of sea creatures, testimony to the time, millions of years ago, when the Andes thrust up through the sea bed. The *refugio* is reached either by road, or by descending into the gorge and crossing the Río Volcán over an extremely rickety footbridge below Baños Morales. The German flag is usually flying outside just in case you have any difficulty in identifying the place. If you want to make a reservation or check the hut is open before leaving Santiago, ring 850 1773.

To return to Santiago you have a choice of a bus from Baños Morales (weekends only, check times locally); a bus from El Volcán; or hitching on one of the many lorries from the mines and quarries at Lo Valdes and beyond. They will take you to the edge of Santiago, from where you can catch a bus to the centre.

Practical information

Time/rating   Allow half a day for the journey up to Baños Morales if you catch a bus all the way, and another two to three hours for the walk into the national park. You could return the next day, but if you have time, it is worth spending a little longer. The Camino de Cajón and the Manquehue can both be done as day trips.

Preparations   Before you leave Santiago, it is worth consulting the Club de Andinismo who will give you information on these and other walks. You should take water for the Manquehue climb.

Maps   The IGM in Santiago have 1:50,000 maps of the Cajón del Maipo. Try sheets 3345-7000 (El Volcán) and 3330-7000 (Embalse del Yeso).

Río Clarillo
by Andrew Dixon

For those not wanting to scale 5000 metre peaks with 20 kilogram packs, but still wishing to dabble their toes in a cool mountain stream, this walk is perfect. Starting at the Reserva Nacional Río Clarillo, 40 kilometres southeast of Santiago, this is a pleasant day's walk.

Getting there
By Car/hitching Take Vicuña Mackenna heading south until you reach Puente Alto (30 minutes). Pass straight through *barrio* Puente Alto, continuing on in the direction of Isla de Pirque. Shortly after crossing Río Maipo at Puente San Ramón, you will come to a T intersection. Turn to the right, passing the famous Concha y Toro vineyard where you might like to stop off on the way home for a tasting to revive yourself. (Open Monday to Saturday, 10.00am to 1.00pm and 3.00pm to 5.00pm.)

Less than one kilometre further on, turn to the left following the signs to El Principal. The road crosses Río Clarillo and degenerates into a gravel road. Five and a half kilometres further on, you will come to an intersection with a small store on one corner. Turn to the left into Calle Nueva and follow this road for another kilometre before turning to the left into Camino El Chalaco. From here it is six kilometres to the park entrance where you will have to pay $1.50 per person to enter. Enter the park and follow the road past the park headquarters (four and a half kilometres from the park entrance) until you see a sign marked *Rodeo*. Turn to the right and at the top of this rise the road ends and the trail begins.

By Bus Buses to Puente Alto leave from Alameda regularly. The trip takes about 45 minutes. From Puente Alto, *colectivos* leave roughly every 15-20 minutes, depending on demand, from Plaza de Puente Alto. Not all of these enter the park, so make sure you get one that does. Buses depart for El Principal regularly but they do not go into the park.

Directions
The park is open from 8.00am to 8.00pm, and no overnight camping is permitted. Officially access is limited beyond a relatively small area near the park entrance, usually full of families and barbeques or *asados* in summer. Access to walk further into the national park can be gained officially by contacting CONAF who will provide you with a Spanish-speaking guide on an appointed

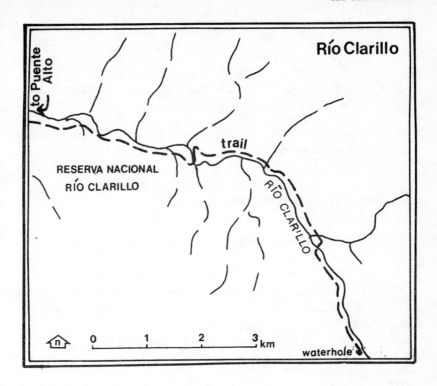

day. Unofficially, the park rangers do not mind you following the trail past the restricted area, provided you do not camp, light fires or destroy the native bush. For the first few kilometres, this path is well used and easy to follow. It begins on the righthand side of the river and crosses back and forth several times, so be prepared to get your feet wet. These crossings are sometimes difficult to find because the spring snow-melt washes the path away.

After one hour, the path comes to another river crossing and it then climbs quite steeply away from the river through a type of almost tropical forest. At the top of this rise, you will join a well-worn, wide track, originally a donkey trail used for transporting firewood from the area. This track continues on the lefthand side of the river and, after crossing a smaller tributary of Río Clarillo, drops back down to cross Río Clarillo again. Another hour along this track and you will arrive at a deep waterhole with its own natural, slippery dip. This is an excellent place to have lunch and cool off. Return back by the same route.

Practical information

Time/rating This walk can be done all year around although it would be very cold to take a dip in the river during the winter months. There and back, it should take between five and six hours. No special equipment or clothes are necessary and upstream the water can be drunk directly from the river.

Maps IGM sheets in the 1:50,000 series San José de Maipo 3330-7015 and San Bernardo 3330-7030; or in the 1:250,000 series: San José de Maipo 3300-6900.

Cerros San Ramón and Provincia
by Andrew Dixon

The most striking feature of Santiago is its backdrop. Unfortunately on most days the Andes or *cordillera* are not visible through the thick smog that hangs over the city. If they are visible, the peaks that will stand out most clearly are Cerros San Ramón (3249m) and Provincia (2713m) or the *precordillera*. Climb to the top of these peaks and you will appreciate how bad the smog really is. It does, however, have one advantage in that it produces blazing red sunsets.

Getting there

From Santiago, take the road to Farellones which intersects with Av. Las Condes about half an hour from the city centre. The intersection of Av. Las Condes and El Camino Farellones can be reached by taking a Las Condes bus from Alameda or an Arrayán *colectivo*. From this intersection it is easy to hitchhike. Five kilometres along this road, about 100 metres before Puente Ñilhue, there is a dirt road off to the right. 300 metres along here you will find a path which climbs steeply and heads straight up the ridge. This ridge will lead you all the way up to Cerro Provincia. If you have a car you should be able to leave it at one of the houses near the start of the walk.

Directions

After about one hour following the path up the ridge, you will come across a small man-made canal. It goes underground for a short while here so be sure you do not walk straight over the top of it as it is the only guaranteed running water supply on this walk. It is best accessed from the lefthand side of the ridge. After about another half hour of walking, you will come to a large tree which is an excellent place to camp if you have set off late in the day.

The path from here is well worn and winds up slowly along the ridge for another hour. To the right, you may see the odd condor soaring in the currents that also carry the noises of the bustling city below. The path then starts to climb quite steeply up to the peak, which you can reach after a further three to four hours. The peak provides excellent views over the *cordillera* and the brown haze that hangs over Santiago.

If you wish to walk on to Cerro San Ramón, continue along this same ridge (fronting Santiago). The ridge climbs up and down and in parts is quite rocky. Nevertheless you will find it easier to follow this than try to walk around the steep sides. Up until early summer, there is often a snow drift below an unnamed peak (2972 metres), about two and a half hours from Cerro Provincia, where you will be able to obtain some water, but do not rely on it being there. About another two hours' walking takes you to the top of Cerro San Ramón.

Practical information
Time/rating Cerro Provincia can be climbed in about eight to ten hours with backpacks. This walk is best done between September and May. Without backpacks it can be climbed in six hours. Allow another three hours to climb back down.

From Cerro Provincia, allow four to five hours with backpacks to reach Cerro San Ramón.

Preparations Some warm clothing to put on at night, a good sleeping bag and a couple of large water bottles are essential. In the middle of summer you can manage without a tent as it very rarely rains, however it will provide you with some protection from the cold. The greatest difficulty you will have with this walk is carrying the volume of water you will need. There is only one water supply, about an hour from the walk's start.

Maps IGM sheets in the 1:50,000 series: Farellones 3315-7015 and San José de Maipo 3330-7015; or in the 1:250,000 series: San José de Maipo 3300-6900.

Villa Paulina to Cerros Paloma and Altar
by Andrew Dixon

Villa Paulina is a small national park hidden in the *cordillera*, only 45 kilometres from Santiago. From here you can walk to the base of a glacier in a day, or for the more adventurous begin a three or

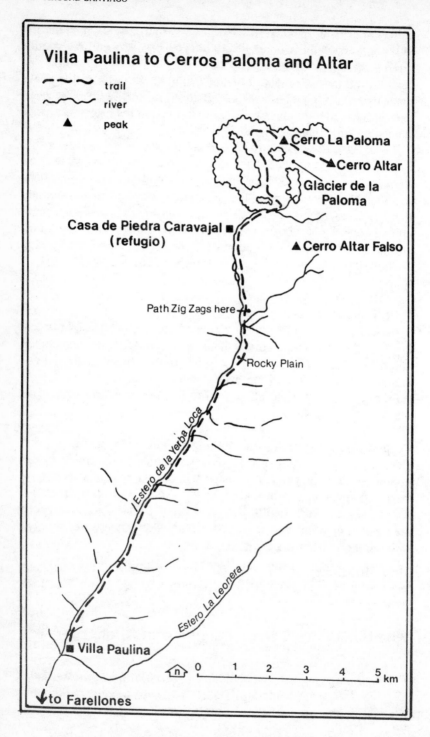

Villa Paulina to Cerros Paloma and Altar

- – – – trail
- ‿‿‿ river
- ▲ peak

▲ Cerro La Paloma

➤ Cerro Altar

Glacier de la Paloma

Casa de Piedra Caravajal ■
(refugio)

▲ Cerro Altar Falso

Path Zig Zags here

Rocky Plain

Estero de la Yerba Loca

Estero La Leonera

■ Villa Paulina

n 0 1 2 3 4 5 km

↓ to Farellones

four day expedition to Cerros Paloma (4930m) and Altar (5222m). There are excellent camping sites at Villa Paulina and beside the river further into the park.

Estero de la Yerba Loca (stream of the crazy grass), obtains its name from a native grass which, if eaten, reportedly can cause a permanent state of delirium. So whilst it is advisable not to nibble the local flora, there is plenty of fresh water to quench your thirst.

Getting there

By car From Santiago, take the road to Farellones which intersects with Av. Las Condes, about half an hour from the city centre. Soon after the turnoff to Miña La Disputada the road begins a series of hairpin bends (40 in all to Farellones). The road to Villa Paulina is on bend 15 (the bends are numbered). Take the rough track from here, and follow it for four kilometres.

By bus There are no buses to Farellones during the summer. Hitches to at least bend 16 are easily obtained from the intersection of Av. Las Condes and El Camino Farellones. To get to the intersection, take an Arrayán *colectivo* or a Las Condes bus from Alameda.

Directions Villa Paulina is no more than the National Park headquarters. Entrance to the park costs $0.60 and there is a $1.50 camping fee. It has plenty of fresh water and level camp sites; however, no supplies can be purchased.

From the park headquarters follow the road (no vehicle access) on the righthand side of the river. It soon degenerates into a well-worn foot track.

The path is marked occasionally by red splashes of paint and is not very difficult to follow. It climbs gradually, meandering through a number of small meadows. Any of these are ideal for camping, although you might find yourself spending the night with a pack of wild horses or a herd of llamas.

After about three and a half hours walking, you will arrive at a rocky plain where the river, tainted by mineral deposits, has coloured the rocks a bright orange. The path now begins to climb more steeply and crosses two small streams sourced by some spectacular peaks to the right — Cerro Altar Falso (4650m) being the highest. Shortly after crossing the second of these two streams, the path zig zags up over a rock wall. Near the top of this rise the path splits; the righthand fork leads to Altar Falso and the lefthand one continues up the valley to Refugio Casa de Piedra Caravajal and Cerros Paloma and Altar.

Casa de Piedra Caravajal is on the lefthand side of the river at the top of this rise. As the name suggests, this is a stone *refugio* with a tin roof and even a small makeshift wooden stove. It is very basic, but provides some protection from the wind. You will find it warmer if you camp in a tent. From here it is one hour to the base of the glacier or two days to Cerros Paloma and Altar.

The path beyond Casa de Piedra Caravajal is less well worn and, therefore, somewhat more difficult to follow. Follow it back over to the righthand side of the river and continue following it up the valley. After climbing past some cascades, the path will begin to head left. At this point, cross back over the river and head for the lefthand side of the glacier. Initially, no path exists because the river washes it away every spring. The path to the right leads to a more difficult route up Cerro Altar.

This river is the last source of running water, so if you are going on to the peaks you will need to stock up here. Water can only be obtained higher up by melting snow. Shortly after crossing the river you will come across some ruins of a wooden *refugio* and a number of areas to camp.

The normal route to Cerro Paloma takes between 15 and 20 hours from the base of the glacier. It is therefore necessary to camp for at least one night before making it to the top. Follow the valley to the left of the glacier, then climb quite steeply up to the east/west ridge formed by Cerros Paloma and Altar (five to six hours).

The best location to camp before proceeding to the peak is on the northern side of this ridge. From this camp site, cross the glacier Paloma and follow the ridge up to the peak (about five hours and another two if you continue along the ridge to Cerro Altar). You will need crampons, ice-axes and a safety rope to cross the glacier. The crossing is not technically difficult, though you will need to exercise caution. Return to Villa Paulina by retracing your steps.

It is possible to climb these peaks from the northern side starting at the mine, Miña La Disputada. This route is a lot shorter and starts at an altitude of 3300 metres. At the time of writing, the company which owns the mine, Exxon, was not allowing public access. They are, however, planning to grant access in the future. The person to contact is Señor Guillermo Garcia (tel 223 3037). Details of the route can be obtained from the Federación de Andinismo (see page 48).

Practical information

Time/rating   Weather permitting, Cerro Paloma can be climbed in three days. Allow an extra half day if you wish to continue on to Cerro Altar. The best time of the year to climb these peaks is between November and April. Only experienced walkers should attempt to climb to the peaks.

For day walkers the return trip to Refugio Casa de Piedra Caravajal takes between seven and eight hours plus another two hours if you wish to climb to the base of the glacier. This day trip can be done all year round.

Preparations   Day walkers should carry a good parka, balaclava and long trousers irrespective of the season as it can be very cold and windy near the glacier.

Groups climbing to Cerros Paloma and Altar will need to carry crampons, ice-axes and a safety rope in order to cross the glacier. See *Camping supplies*, page 46, for details of where to rent such equipment. All supplies should be purchased in Santiago.

Maps   IGM sheets in the 1:50,000 series: Farellones 3315-7015 and La Disputada 3300-7017; or in the 1:250,000 series: San José de Maipo 3300-6900.

Cerro Plomo
by Andrew Dixon

> There comes a time it is the beginning of manhood or womanhood when one realizes that adventure is as humdrum as routine unless one assimilates it, unless one relates it to a central core which grows within and gives it contour and significance.
> *Lewis Munford.*

From Santiago looking east towards the *cordillera* on a clear day, one peak stands out behind all the others. It is one of those peaks that inspires adventurers. A rounded white mass, Cerro Plomo's attraction is due largely to its awesome height of 5430 metres and its accessibility from Santiago. Technically this is not a difficult peak to climb. The only problems you are likely to have will be with the altitude.

Cerro Plomo is also famous because an Inca mummy was found just below the peak. Still in very good condition, the mummy is now housed in the Museo Nacional de Histórico Natural in Parque Quinta Normal in Santiago. So whilst you climb to the top with

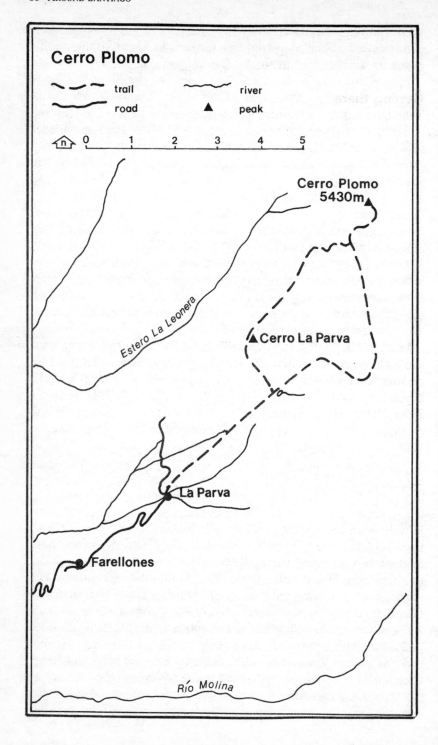

your space-age rucksack, super-snug sleeping bag and gortex wind jacket, give some thought to the Incas who walked these trails centuries before with little more than colourful ponchos.

Getting there

Take the road to Farellones, which intersects with Av. Las Condes about half an hour from the city centre. From this intersection it is relatively easy to hitch at least as far as Farellones. Continue on from Farellones by road for a couple of miles to the ski resort, La Parva.

Directions

From La Parva follow the ski lifts up the lefthand side of the mountain in the direction of the pass, to the right of Falsa Parva. There is a small lagoon just on the other side of this ridge which makes an ideal place to camp if you started late in the day. From here, you can either follow the ridge formed by Cerros Falsa Parva, La Parva, Pintor and Leonera, or climb directly down into Cajón del Cepo ravine and follow Río Molina.

The advantage of the former is that it is more direct and will prepare you better for the altitude; the disadvantage is that there is no running water until you reach the *refugio* (seven to eight hours). If you take the La Parva route from the pass, follow the ridge up to Falsa Parva (3740 metres) passing by Cerro La Parva on the Santiago side, and on up to Cerro Pintor (4220 metres). Shortly after you have reached this, you will need to climb back down a scree slope and into the Cajón del Cepo. This route is relatively easy to follow except for finding where to climb back down. At the bottom you will find a small orange *refugio* close to the river.

The alternative route, following Cajón del Cepo and Río Molina is well worn and easy to follow. It is relatively easy walking and there is plenty of water on the way. However it will take some eight to ten hours to reach the *refugio* from the pass just below Falsa Parva. If you would rather break this up into two days, there are good grassy places to camp at Piedra Numerada (four hours from the pass), a huge rock covered in numbers, beside the river.

From the orange *refugio*, it is five to six hours to the peak. The path climbs up a scree on the righthand side of the river. At the base of glacier Esmeralda (4500 metres) you can camp and have spectacular views of the glacier. *Be careful* to do so on high land as this basin floods on a hot day. The path continues up on the righthand side of the glacier and after another hour you will come to *refugio* Agostini, at an altitude of 4700 metres. This *refugio* has been partially destroyed by the elements. No running water is available here but you should be able to find snow to melt. The path from here zig zags up a steep scree.

Just before reaching the top of this false peak, the path turns to the left. A little further on you will find an Inca monument. From here you need to use your crampons to cross the glacier. Follow the ridge up to the peak of Cerro Plomo. Take great care crossing the glacier as there are a number of cracks which you might fall down.

NOTE: Only set off from the orange *refugio* to climb to the top in fine weather. When climbing back down, take the route which follows Cajón del Cepo, past Piedra Numerada. This hike should only be attempted by climbers experienced with ropes, crampons and ice-axes.

Practical information

Time/rating   This walk can be done in three days although you are well advised to allow up to four days to give you more time to adjust to the altitude. The best time of the year is between November and April. From May to September you will need cross country skis as you will be walking in snow at least one metre deep.

Preparations   Supplies should be purchased in Santiago, as very little is available in Farellones or La Parva during the summer months. A sturdy tent and good sleeping bag are essential as it can become extremely cold and windy at night. It has been known to snow in the middle of summer so you need to be prepared for all conditions. A gas stove will suffice, but it will take some time to boil water due to the altitude. Crampons and ice-axes are essential for crossing the glacier at the top. A safety rope is also advisable. See *Camping Supplies*, page 46, for information on where to rent equipment.

Maps   IGM sheets in the 1:50,000 series Farellones 3315-7015, 3315-7000 and 3300-7000; or in the 1:250,000 series San José de Maipo 3300-6900.

TOWARDS VIÑA DEL MAR
The Cerro la Campaña National Park

by Hamish Galpin

Chile's central chain of mountains, which run parallel to the coast and the Andes, rise to around 2000 metres northwest of Santiago and are easily accessible by road, bus and even rail. Cerro La Campaña (1900m), within the park of the same name, is a sharply-peaked mountain which rises directly from the Aconcagua valley and dominates the area around it. Cerro La Campaña is clearly visible as the highest mountain in the range to the north of the main Santiago-Valparaíso/Viña road as its passes through the forests near the coast.

An outing here is an ideal day trip if you are relaxing in Viña del Mar for a few days. It is also an excellent way to prepare for more arduous treks and climbs in the Andes. As well as offering 1700 metres of ascent, there are good routes on the 200 metres south-facing cliffs below the summit and these can be approached to within 15 minutes walk by jeep track.

Getting there
By bus or train Perhaps the most rewarding way to approach this national park is from Viña del Mar. Here you can take either the local bus or metropolitan railway and travel through attractive countryside and small towns to the bottom of the mountain at Limache. Darwin may well have followed a similar route when he explored the area and climbed the mountain in 1836. Limache buses are also marked Olmue, a small village just west of Limache where you get off.

Buses depart frequently from Viña del Mar from the road running alongside the river channel, on the opposite bank from the main square and tourist office. Trains depart less frequently from the other side of the main square. Journey times: train one hour to Limache, then bus/taxi; bus one and a half hours all the way to the park.

By car/hitching The Carretera Panamericana passes by the north side of the mountain, eight kilometres south of the town, La Calera, where it crosses the Río Aconcagua. To get to the official park entrance at Olmue, you must drive round the west side of the mountain through Quillota. The jeep track, mentioned above, takes you through the park, crossing two ridges before descending to meet the carretera in the Aconcagua valley, eight kilometres south of La Calera.

Directions

Walk through Olmue and after a few minutes, you will arrive at the gateway to the park (entrance fee $1). There is a small cafe at the bus terminus which has a diagram of the climbing routes. From here, the mountain is clearly visible, the steep left (northwest) ridge providing an exciting scramble and the right (southeast) ridge the walker's route. A jeep track and a well-maintained path climb through dense woodland which thins during ascent, giving way to thick shrubbery and stunted beech trees.

The path crosses the track several times and joins it after about three hours. Follow the track up an easy gradient to a plateau where camping and parking are possible. The jeep track climbs from the plateau over the northwest ridge several hundred feet below the summit.

For the scramble, you should follow the track to this high point. From here, you will need to pick the best possible route up the broad ridge, over rocky terrain that is covered in scrub and dead brush, before the final 200 metre scramble. This looks ominous at first, but by sticking to the ridge as much as possible, you should pick up the yellow arrows on the rock that indicate the route to the summit.

The main path continues directly upwards from the plateau through thin beech woods and then traverses diagonally upwards, below the cliffs, weaving around large boulders to reach the southeast ridge. From here the path climbs above tree level and there is some loose rock and scree to negotiate before reaching the top. The graffiti-covered summit provides an unwelcome splash of colour, but the panoramic view is splendid if there is little haze.

Practical information

Time/ratings Allow about four hours for the ascent and two hours for the descent.

Preparations Take water as availability is scarce during the walk. Take food too if you are going direct to the park as the cafe has little to take away.

Camping, accommodation and other amenities can be found in Olmue and Limache, including an ample supply of beer from the local brewery! There is also a music festival in the summer.

Map IGM Sheet in the 1:100,000 series: Quillota - Quillota y Válparaíso 4116.

Chapter Eight

Araucanía region, Chile

by Christine and John Myerscough, updated by Patrick Symington

The Indians first, by novelty dismayed,
As Gods revered us, and as Gods obeyed;
But when they found we were of woman born,
Their homage turned to enmity and scorn.
Ercilla, *La Araucana.*

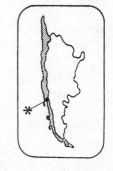

Introduction

When the Spanish *conquistador* Pedro de
Valdivia pushed south from Santiago in search of
new territory, he was forced to stop at the
settlement to which he had given his name after
facing resistance from the fierce Araucanian Indians. In 1554 the
Indians, who in their own tongue call themselves Mapuches,
meaning 'people of the earth', captured Valdivia and tortured him
to death. For 300 years the area in which the Indians lived remained
impenetrable and it was not until 1881 that the Mapuches became
incorporated into the rest of Chile. Of the estimated 20,000 pure
blooded indigenous Indians left in Chile, virtually all live in the
provinces between the Bío-Bío and the Toltén rivers. There are
possibly 150,000 more of mixed blood who are bilingual. The
region's main population centre, Temuco, has the highest
concentration of Indians of any Chilean city.

Much of Araucanía consists of rich fertile lowlands where most of
Chile's wheat and barley are grown, hence its reputation as the
'granary of Chile'. To the west the snow-capped volcanoes of the
Andes tower over glistening lakes. Many of these volcanoes are still
active: in December 1988 about 2000 people had to be evacuated
from the town of Malalcahuello after the 2865-metre Lonquimay
volcano, in the east of the region, erupted. Further south you can
climb the Villarrica volcano and peer into over the crater lip into its
fiery depths of molten lava.

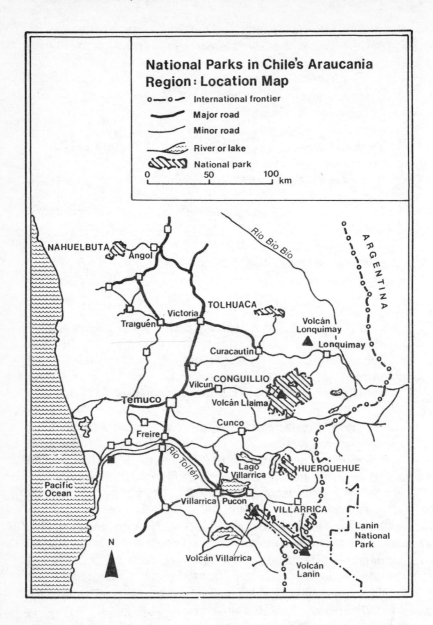

National Parks in Chile's Araucania Region: Location Map

- o——o— International frontier
- Major road
- Minor road
- River or lake
- National park

0   50   100 km

This region also boasts some of the richest temperate forests in the world. Here you will find giant *Araucaria araucana* or monkey puzzle trees, whose distinctive umbrella-like profiles has led to their local name of *paraguas*. Many are believed to be up to 1200 years old. Their nuts are edible and delicious roasted over an open fire. You will also see oak, *coihue*, evergreen beech and larch trees, their trunks decorated with the delightful pink bells of Chile's national flower, the *copihue*.

Fortunately Chileans have preserved the beauty of this region by setting up no fewer than six national parks, administered by CONAF. Each has well marked paths, information centres and basic facilities (some have more than just the basics). Several weeks could be spent enjoying these parks.

The main centre for visiting the parks is Temuco (220,000 inhabitants). If you want to find out more about the Mapuche Indians, you can visit Temuco's Araucanía Museum at Alemania 84. Temuco is also the best place in Chile to buy Mapuche handicrafts such as woollen ponchos, pullovers and blankets. The handicrafts market is on the corner of Diego Portales and Aldunate, or there is a Galería Artesanal at the junction of Balmaceda and Bulnes. Information on the national parks can be obtained from the CONAF office or from the tourist office at Calle Bulnes 586, on the corner with Claro Solar.

Pucón and Villarrica National Park and volcano

The base for making the climb up Volcán Villarrica is the resort town of Pucón on the shores of Lago Villarrica, a half day journey from Temuco. This offers a variety of accommodation from simple family pensions to the luxurious Gran Hotel to a beautiful camp site beside the lake.

Volcán Villarrica (2840 metres) is Chile's most active volcano. An eruption in 1971 destroyed the village of Conaripe when molten lava, pouring out of an opening in the rim, melted part of the icecap and caused vast avalanches of hot mud mixed with boulders and trees to descend on the village (a similar disaster occurred in Colombia in 1985). The last eruption was in 1984.

The volcano can be climbed up and down in eight hours, but unfortunately, as a result of a number of accidents and, more seriously, deaths you now must prove to the Chilean police that you are experienced and sufficiently well equipped to tackle the climb if you are not taking a guide. A number of agencies in Pucón make regular pilgrimages to the summit for a fee of $35-45 including the entrance fee to the park ($6). Some agencies do not offer a refund if a trip is cancelled due to inclement weather. Also beware of unoffical guides. For information about the state of the climb, ask the park guards.

Good boots, crampons, ice-axes, sunglasses and suntan cream are essential. They can be hired in Pucón from the bicycle shop on Calle Palguin, near the fire station. Cars or jeeps can be hired for the stretch of road leading to the car park, just below the ski centre. This is where the walk begins. You can sleep in the *refugio*, just inside the park, but it is badly in need of renovation or you can camp in the camp site in the woods just below.

To start the climb, follow the stanchions for the ski lift up the loose volcanic grit. When these end, head straight for the summit across the glacier. Towards the top the ice gives way to old lava flows, which give good grip although they are quite sharp to walk on. The view over the crater is an unforgettable experience, and you can climb down into the caldera. The volcano's sulphurous fumes, however, can be quite nauseous. We found a half lemon held to the nose and mouth in a handkerchief helped.

After your climb you could relax in a hot bath in one of the many thermal pools in the area. The two most popular and developed are the Termas de Huife, 33 kilometres east of Pucón, and the Termas de Palguín, 28 kilometres southeast of Pucón. Both can be reached by bus from Pucón. We, however, bathed in a picturesque family-run pool on a bend in the river about ten kilometres before Huife called Quimay-Co. It has good camping facilities in the woods above the river, and small huts for hire. From Quimay-Co it is an easy day's walk along quiet lanes to Huerquehue National Park.

Huerquehue National Park

Huerquehue National Park, 100 kilometres southeast of Temuco and 35 kilometres from Pucón, can be reached from Pucón by taking a bus in the direction of Lago Caburga and asking to be dropped at the school at the junction for the park, otherwise known as Paillaco. You will have to walk the last seven kilometres to the park entrance.

The park encompasses a profusion of small lakes. The first you come to is Lago Tinquilco. On its eastern shore there is a lovely camp site with a dozen pitches each with table, benches and a barbeque pit. Note that camping is only permitted in designated camp sites. You may be able to buy *pan casero* (homemade bread) and basic supplies from some of the farms along the way. From the information centre you can make the walk to Lagunas Verde, Toro,

Chico and Clara. The trail takes you past a farm where cold drinks can be bought, then climbs steeply through bamboo forest. Although the signpost says the walk is only five kilometres, it took us a hot two and a half hours, but it is well worth the effort.

From here there are trails which take you further into the park. Consult the *guardaparque* if you wish to do this, as he is well acquainted with the park's many walking possibilities.

"It is worth going up to the pass by Lago Huerquehue where there is a spectacular Araucaria forest. From Laguna Verde a path climbs Cerro Comulu from where there is a fine view to Lanín volcano.

"The Tromen Pass crosses the border between Pucón and Junin de los Andes. If you get off the bus at the Argentine checkpost and asks permission, you can climb **Lanín**. There is a *refugio* half way up. Ice-axe and crampons would be needed for the full ascent." (P. Frew)

Nahuelbuta National Park

Set in the magnificent Nahuelbuta mountain range, this park is famous for its abundant monkey puzzle trees draped with old man's beard lichens. Situated in the northwest of Araucanía, 35 kilometres west of the town of Angol, it includes 20 kilometres of footpaths, the 1560-metre Cerro Nahuel and a number of camp sites. In summer buses run from Angol to the park.

Tolhuaca National Park

This is reached from the town of Curacautín, 44 kilometres to the south. It has camping facilities next to Laguna Malleco (which offers good fishing) and five footpaths covering 24 kilometres of trails. A worthwhile walk is to the spectacular Salto de Malleco, a 50-metre waterfall.

Eight kilometres south of the park are the popular Termas de Tolhuaca, set in superb scenery, with a camp site and a hotel. You can chose between man-made baths and natural river pools where the water temperature reaches up to 93°F.

Cerro Ñielol National Park

This must be one of the few national parks inside a city. Situated in Temuco, it consists of a beautiful wooded hill with an information centre and a restaurant with magnificent views over the city and its surroundings. An old tree in the park, called La Patagua, marks the spot where the first parliament met to sign a treaty which led to the end of hostilities between the government and the Mapuches in 1881.

Conguillio National Park

Dominating this park, one of the region's most popular, is the spectacular 3050-metre Volcán Llaima whose incredible lava flows have left huge barren swathes through the otherwise forested landscape. There are a number of attractive lakes, the largest of which, Laguna Conguillio, is connected by underground tunnels through the lava to the Río Trufel Trufel. From the lake you can hike into the Sierra Nevada. At Laguna Verde there is a free camp site without facilities. Equally worth hiking to are the secluded Lagunas Arco, Iris and Captren. In summer buses run from Temuco to Curacautín from where you catch a bus at 6.30pm during the week which takes you to the CONAF hut where you can camp. From here it is a 16 kilometre hike to the information centre at Laguna Conguillio where there are camping facilities ($12 per tent) and boats and chalets for hire.

Chapter Nine

The Lakes District

The Lakes District covers an area of about 300 kilometres from north to south, and straddles the Andes between Argentina and Chile about two thirds of the way down. Lakes, rivers, waterfalls, thermal pools, glaciers and snowfields combine with an astonishing array of vegetation and wildlife to produce one of the most magnificent landscapes in the world. On the east side, in Argentina, the lakes tend to lie between 600 and 1700 metres above sea level and to be cold and wild. On the western side in Chile they are 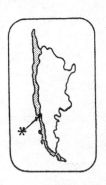 lower, mostly less than 300 metres, and are much warmer and gentler. There are dozens of major lakes and hundreds of minor ones, and each has its own distinct climate and character, but they have in common a sparse population of *estancieros*, *gauchos*, Indians and assorted government employees. It is these hospitable people, as much as the natural wonders, that make backpacking in the Lakes District an unforgettable experience.

The climate is ideal, allowing you to ski in winter and bask in hot sunshine in summer. The best time for walking is between December and March when the tops are clear of snow.

The hikes which follow, centre around three main towns: Valdivia (Chile), Puerto Montt (Chile) and Bariloche (Argentina). In all three can be seen the influence of European immigrants — mainly German — who settled here at the end of last century. A seafood dinner, for instance, may well be rounded off with German *Kuchen* or locally made Swiss chocolate. The thatched or red tiled houses of the rural north are here replaced by frame buildings of north European design, faced with unpainted shingles, high pitched roofs and quaint, ornate balconies.

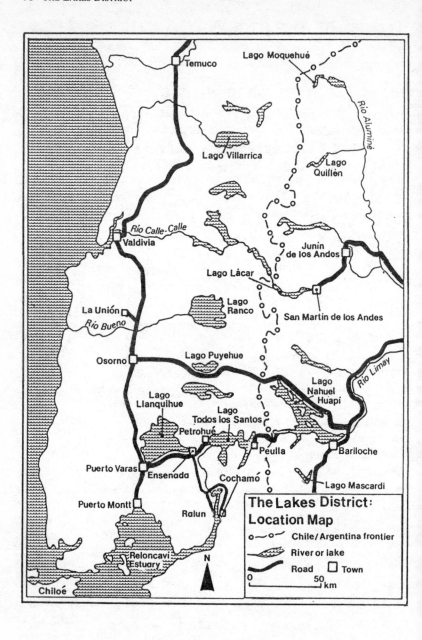

Lago Moquehué

Temuco

Río Aluminé

Lago Villarrica

Lago Quillén

Río Calle-Calle

Valdivia

Junín de los Andes

Lago Lácar

Lago Ranco

San Martín de los Andes

La Unión

Río Bueno

Osorno

Lago Puyehue

Río Limay

Lago Nahuel Huapí

Lago Llanquihue

Lago Todos los Santos

Petrohué

Peulla

Bariloche

Puerto Varas

Ensenada

Cochamó

Lago Mascardi

Puerto Montt

Ralun

The Lakes District: Location Map

o—o—o Chile/Argentina frontier

River or lake

Road ☐ Town

N

0   50 km

Reloncaví Estuary

Chiloé

TOWNS OF THE REGION
Valdivia

Arriving in the area around Valdivia is like stepping into Germany before the First World War: men with Teutonic faces and flat caps, women with headscarves, horses and carts vying with motor traffic on the neat gravel roads through the prim countryside.   The German culture is at its strongest in the dairy farming region between here and Puerto Montt. German colonists first arrived in the mid 19th century and their impact on agriculture, social customs and industry is evident everywhere. The earthquake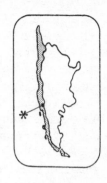
and tidal wave of 1960, however, destroyed most of the 19th century architecture. The Universidad Austral de Chile across the Río Calle-Calle has an attractive campus and cheap meals in the students' canteen. Incidentally, the abundance of youths walking around with shaved heads may make you wonder if the city is a centre for Hare Krishna followers. Apparently the haircut is not a result of religious fervour but of an initiation ceremony performed on first year students by their peers.

The tourist office, at Calle Arturo Prat 555, by the dock, provides a good map of the region and local rivers. The railway station is at Ecuador 2000, off Av. Picarte and the bus terminal is at Muñoz and Arturo Prat, by the river.

Puerto Montt

Over 1000 kilometres from Santiago, this is the southernmost stop of the railway and an embarkation point for boats going south. For romantics this alone would make it worth seeing, but its location among lush rolling hills and its quaint old shingle-fronted buildings give it a Nordic charm which captivates everyone. Incidentally, it also offers the greatest variety of seafood in the whole of South America.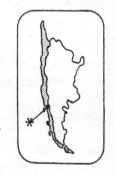

Most of the town's attractions are on the seafront. From the Plaza de Armas follow Avenida Diego Portales (the Costanera) west, past the raw seafood stalls opposite the bus station to the offices of Empresa Marítima del Estado (Empremar). Here you can get passages to the southern fjords, the island of Chiloé, Punta Arenas and even Antarctica should you wish. Just beyond the naval base is the office of the Gobernación Marítima where you can find out where the smaller boats are going. Continue past warehouses stacked with wine and cereals and you will come to Angelmó, a gourmet's paradise of tiny restaurants serving seafood of every description. Much of the seafood is raw, although a cooked version is usually available for weaker stomachs. Angelmó is a good place to buy Chilean handicrafts, sweaters and so on. They are much cheaper than further north, although the place has become rather touristy and the quality of some of the goods has dropped. From the end of the waterfront you can be rowed for a few pesos across the narrow channel to the wooded island of Tenglo, a favourite place for picnics, where the *curanto* (seafood, meat and vegetable stew) is reputedly the best in Chile. From the cross at the top you get magnificent views of Puerto Montt and Volcán Osorno.

The tourist office is at Edif. Intendencia Regional, Av. Décima Región, or at the kiosk in the Plaza de Armas. Rail station at San Felipe 50. Empremar offices at Av. Diego Portales 1450. Navimag, Terminal Transbordadores Angelmó.

An agency in Angelmó can advise on all aspects of hiking in the Lakes District and organizes tailor-made treks. The office is on Av. Angelmó 2270 (postal address Casilla 854), tel/fax 258 555.

If you want to travel between Puerto Montt and Puerto Natales for the Torres del Paine National Park and the Serrano glaciers, Navimag operates the *M/N Puerto Eden*. A one-way trip on the vessel takes four days, and the company has a special economy fare for backpackers. All fares include three meals a day, and vary between US$213 (low season) and US$425 (high season, November to April). The standard economy fare is US$128. Navimag's office is at Avenida Angelmó 2187 (tel 253 318/fax 258 540).

San Carlos de Bariloche

San Carlos de Bariloche, Argentina's answer to Chamonix, nestles on a narrow shelf beneath Cerro Otto with a fantastic view over Lago Nahuel Huapí, the biggest of the region's lakes. An unashamedly tourist town, its only manufacturing industries are chocolates, jams and woolly sweaters. Its population of 70,000 is almost entirely employed in catering for visitors, a highly lucrative and successful occupation. In consequence the town gets terribly noisy and overcrowded in high season and it is far better to visit out of season in

spring or autumn when the temperature is pleasant. Bariloche was once the haunt of Nazi war criminals, but today it is about as likely a haunt for war criminals as Aviemore or Aspen.

The chances are you will end up spending at least a few days in Bariloche, and if you have just staggered in from several weeks in the mountains you will probably find it a nice change. Hotels are expensive so the best option is to rent a room in somebody's house. Ask the Tourist Office in the Centro Cívico to help you.

Information on national parks at San Martín 24, or from Sociedad Profesional de Guías de Turismo, Casilla de Correo 51, 8400 Bariloche. Trekking information from Club Andino Bariloche, Calle 20 de Febrero 30. Details about train services from San Martín 127 (station is five kilometres east of centre).

Getting to the Lakes District
From Santiago
In summer, trains run from Santiago to Temuco and Puerto Montt. The service is not very reliable and takes considerably longer than the bus. On the other hand it is a unique experience especially if you do not mind paying the extra for the sleeper. Some of the sleeper cars date back to the 1930s. Their sumptuous seats of golden velvet and heavy mahogany convert into exceedingly comfortable wide beds. A night between their starched linen sheets is an experience not to be missed. The journey takes you through the heart of Chile's wine country, a landscape very French with long avenues of Lombardy poplars, and during the night you cross the Río Bío-Bío which historically marked the beginning of Indian territory.

Bus services are faster, cheaper and more reliable, but less fun. Buses leave from the Terminal de Buses Santiago, O'Higgins 3878. Tickets from offices all along Morandé. Ladeco and LAN-Chile do flights to the main towns.

From Buenos Aires
Trains leave Constitución Station daily for Bahía Blanca. Unfortunately, only two trains a week continue on to Bariloche and only one a week to Zapala. The 1370-kilometre trip to Zapala takes 26 hours and the 1770-kilometre journey to Bariloche takes at least 31 hours. The landscape is only interesting between Bariloche and Jacobacci (four and a half hours). If this sounds a long time to spend on a dusty train you can go by bus in about two-thirds of the time or by plane in a mere hour or two (provided you can get a seat on a flight).

PUERTO MONTT TO PUERTO NATALES BY BOAT

by Denise Heywood

South of Puerto Montt lies a third of Chile where only three per cent of the population lives. It is a remote region of desolate fjords, canals and uninhabited, thickly forested islands. Every nine days a roll-on/roll-off vehicle ferry, the *Tierra del Fuego*, plies the only route through the gloomy, storm-laden archipelago, 1460 kilometres to Puerto Natales, gateway to Patagonia.

Horror stories abound about the three-day journey on the 'ro/ro', occupied mainly by truck drivers and their 90 vehicles, but it is a unique adventure. There are six first-class cabins and 34 bunks which can be booked in advance, and 97 reclining seats which go on sale four hours before departure, with priority given to the lorry drivers.

We queued until just before departure, got the last two seats and hopped on board. As I sank into my reclining plastic chair, rows of which were wedged in a container placed amidships, with only four toilets to share between all of us, my heart sank even lower and I wanted to jump ship. But when we pulled out through Seno Reloncaví and the Golfo de Ancud, passing isolated lighthouses, symbols of loneliness and human absence, my spirits rose and the brooding mist cleared to give us a spectacular view of Chiloé.

As we slipped through the calm waters of the Golfo de Corcovado and the Archipelago de los Chonos, dolphins leapt up to smile at us, vying with seals and penguins and disporting whales, while colonies of sealions barked from rocky promontories. We spotted skimmers and flocks of shearwaters gliding close to the waves, while their relatives, petrels and albatrosses, circled the boat continuously. The display of marine and bird life never ceased throughout the journey, animating the greyest seascapes. Our fellow passengers were equally animated, and included 16 different nationalities. We swarmed to the canteen three times a day where the crew dished out palatable fare from spotless galleys. On the second day the crew distributed black plastic bags to everyone and polyglot conversations were reduced to universal moans as the ship pitched for a whole day in lashing rain in the ominously named Golfo de Penas.

When the ship returned to the fjords and pale passengers resurfaced, we edged silently another 250 nautical miles past the historically named Angostura Inglesa and Isla Wellington to Puerto Eden. This desolate fishing town is home to 300 Alacalufe Indians who sailed towards us in their wooden boats to exchange their shellfish for other goods, their only contact with the outside world.

On the last night the moon shone and we abandoned our reclining chairs to dance the lambada and drink *pisco* sours with our tiny, mustachioed Captain. But at 4.00am, as the ship negotiated the narrow 40 metre Kirke canal, cut through high rock where the slack water is only 30 minutes between tides, she ran aground with a crunch that resounded from bow to stern. With a huge hole in her hull she chugged into Puerto Natales at dawn. We tired revellers scuttled ashore like rats, sobered by the biting wind, and left our memorable captain and crew to an uncertain fate.

A HIKE IN THE NORTHERN LAKES
by John Pilkington

This walk takes you past some of the remotest and arguably finest lakes in Argentina's northern Lakes District. You will pass through forests of giant *lenga* and *araucaria* (monkey puzzle) trees, and catch tantalizing glimpses of the Lanín and Llaima volcanoes. These provide a home to interesting wildfowl and animals such as *ciervos* (European red deer) and *jabalís* (wild pigs). You will walk through upland pampas where gauchos bring their horses, sheep and cattle to graze on the long summer grass. The only other humans are a few *guardaparques* and frontier guards at the *gendarmerías*. Otherwise you will probably have the place to yourself.

The walk, although not long (80 kilometres at most), is tough and not to be taken lightly. The trail varies from clear to elusive to non-existent, and a compass is vital. Although the hike can be done in three days, some of the spots are so good that you will want to linger, and you should take supplies for five days or more, since there are none en route. Check in with the *guardaparque* and frontier guards at each lake: apart from being interesting people who can tell you a lot about the wildlife, trail conditions, weather, etc, they are linked by radio and can send a search party if you miss a rendezvous.

Since the lakes are separated by rows of mountains the hike inevitably involves a lot of up and down. But from the ridges you will see some of the extraordinary highlights of the northern Lakes District: aerial views of the lakes packed in between steep wedges of the Andes; the peaks of the Catan-Lil range on the eastern horizon which look as if they are out of *Lord of the Rings*; the strange vertical outcrops of Cerro Iglesias and the 'Giant Causeway'; and of course those perfectly shaped volcanoes. The highest point on the walk, at the top of the first pass, is less than 2000 metres — mild stuff if you have just come from Peru or Bolivia — but a steep climb all the same. The other passes are both about 1500 metres and much easier.

Camp sites abound, both by the lakes and in the upland pampas. There are also a number of unoccupied rough shelters where you can spend the night. All along the trail there is fresh, clean water and plenty of dead wood for making campfires. You will also see

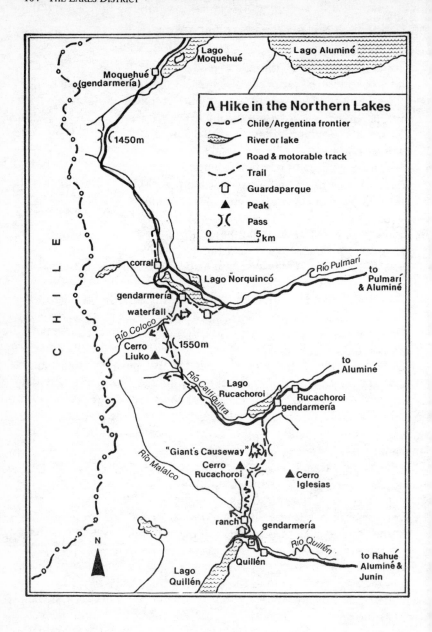

A Hike in the Northern Lakes

○—○— Chile/Argentina frontier

River or lake

Road & motorable track

- - - Trail

⌂ Guardaparque

▲ Peak

)(Pass

0 ——————— 5 km

a common lichen which is making dinner of most of the region's timber. You would be doing the trees a favour if you harvested this useless and destructive mould for use as bedding, kindling or toilet paper (admittedly a bit scratchy in the last function).

Like all the hikes in the Lakes District, this is best done in summer from December to March. It is passable in November and April, but the rest of the year is blocked by snow.

Getting there

The walk starts at Quillén at the entrance to the Lanín National Park in Argentina. If coming from Zapala, take Route 46 southwest to Rahué, a junction settlement south of Aluminé. On the way you will pass Laguna Blanca, in bleak, eerie desert country, which in summer serves as a pitstop for large numbers of northern hemisphere birds such as Canada geese. No buses run this route, but hitchhiking should be easy.

If coming from the south, take the main San Martín to Zapala road and turn off along the road to Rahué and Aluminé. The turning is five kilometres north of Junín de los Andes just after the bridge over the Río Chimehuín. Hitchhiking from the junction is quite easy.

Alternatively you can take a bus from Junín to Rahué and Aluminé. From Rahué follow Route 46 west for 30 kilometres to the village of Quillén. From here it is about a kilometre to the entrance to Lanín National Park and the *gendarmería*, a kilometre beyond which lies Lago Quillén.

The broken finger shaped lake is a marvel when the sun shines, and positively satanic when it is stormy, as it often is. Straight down the first run of the lake is the pointed white wizard's hat of Volcán Lanín which, flanked by more humble ridges on either side of the lake, makes a magician's court presiding over the magic, transparent table of the lake.

On the south side, above its first knuckle, is a rock formation sitting on a peak, the stones bent so as to resemble a tiny troll sitting on his master's cap watching the mystical proceedings. (The rocks' etherial qualities, however, seen to have been lost on the local Indians who gave them the undignified name of 'Pile of Dog Shit.') Where the road meets the lake is an excellent place for camping, sunbathing and gathering your strength for the walk ahead.

Directions

When you have had your fill of the soft life, go and see the *guardaparque* in the big house overlooking the lake. He has good maps of the area (framed, unfortunately, so you cannot take them away) and the trail starts in his back yard. For the first hour the trail is wide and unmistakable, heading first east and then north to a ranch by the Río Malalco, a tributary of the Río Quillén. Beyond the ranch it peters out for several hundred metres so, if you can, get a *gaucho* to show you where it picks up again. Otherwise, ford the river opposite the ranch and look for two side valleys ahead. The trail goes straight up the spur between the two, through thorn bushes, wild bamboo and then a forest of those amazing monkey puzzle trees. The trail is steep, but the view which opens up behind is a good reward, especially when Volcán Lanín reappears.

Three hours beyond the ranch, near a pile of rocks, the trail suddenly levels out and for the next hour you more or less contour the side of the righthand valley to the corrie at its head. There is good camping here, with plenty of flat grassy spots and tinkling, ice cold streams.

The trail leaves the corrie on its east side, at right angles to the way you came in, just right of a large area of scrub. It soon becomes faint again, but the pass is clear enough: just keep heading due east until you reach it. The top is a place to rest and admire, for not only are the snows of Cerro Rucachoroi and Volcán Lanín still in full view behind, but the spires of Cerro Iglesias and the whole of the Catan-Lil range are now visible to the east. You would do well to take breath here: the way ahead becomes difficult to follow and soon disappears in a bog.

From the pass, contour the hillside to your left as far as a spur or headland, which you should reach in about 45 minutes. Now take a long, hard look at the bog ahead. Your route is through the low pass which you can see beyond, about 20 degrees east of magnetic north, but if it has been raining recently the best way to reach it is probably to continue contouring the hillside to your left. If not, strike cheerfully across the bog and say your prayers.

At the second pass you will come across a remarkable pile of granite rocks, whose best imitation (though with inferior materials) is the Giant's Causeway in Ireland. Here change course from 20 degrees east to 20 degrees west of magnetic north and soon you will find yourself following a stream. The valley in which lies Lago Rucachoroi, your next lake, is straight ahead, although you will not see the lake for another hour. Keeping the stream to your right, follow it down through thorn bushes and a grove of monkey puzzle trees until it veers away to the right. Then strike out on a bearing of 30 degrees west of north until you see the lake. It is everyone for themselves now: scramble down the hillside any way you can and follow the lakeside track to the *gendarmería* and *guardería* two thirds of the way down the lake. A couple of kilometres beyond is the tiny Indian village of Rucachoroi. There are no shops, so once you have bidden farewell to the boys in blue your best course is to the head of the lake. Here, under a small grove of trees by the lapping waters, is the nicest camp site on the hike.

From Rucachoroi to Ñorquincó the trail follows the wide valley of the Río Calfiquitra for several kilometres before climbing the 1550-metre Cerro Liuko pass to reach the valley of the Río Coloco. For the first couple of hours you pass through flat pampa. Then, after fording the river twice in quick succession, you climb through woodland for about an hour until suddenly another wide flat pampa opens up ahead. Now you will need all your powers of pathfinding because traffic between Rucachoroi and Ñorquincó seems to have declined and the trail over the pass, being hardly used, is suffering from a severe case of *The Day of the Triffids*.

As soon as the pampa comes into view, look for a big rock with a tree on top. The main valley trail passes to the left of this rock, but your route goes to the right, fords the river and heads diagonally across the pampa to a point about 300 metres to the left of a big round boulder on top of a little hill. Where you meet the forest again you will find a clearing with lots of dead wood and a small stream. Cross the stream by the stepping stone and look for the trail at about 75 degrees west of north. It winds up the hill, disappearing now and again in bamboo thickets and under fallen tree trunks, but keeping all the time between 50 degrees and 80 degrees west of north. After an hour or so it emerges into another plain, one kilometre long by half a kilometre wide. This is the summit of the pass. The trail re-enters the forest at the far end. Keeping first right and then left of the stream it descends through the woods.

When you reach the main valley you will join another trail from Quillén, more direct though less scenic, and turn northeast. But do not worry if you miss the junction: the trail is hardly any clearer than the one you are on, and you will find yourself going northeast in any case. Enticing views of Lago Ñorquincó begin to open up ahead, and you will pass wild apple trees and a huge waterfall on the river below. After walking an hour in this direction you will come to a small plain and then a large one, the second just after crossing a tiny stream. Now you must concentrate again, because on the second plain two trails invisibly cross. The one you want leaves the pampa to your left, and re-crosses the small stream a little lower down before heading for the red and white buildings of the *gendarmería* where the main river enters the lake. Its occupants do not see many backpackers, or indeed any other sort of human being, so you can be sure of a warm welcome. We were immediately presented with mugs of wine and offered a camping place in their garden.

The most difficult part of the walk is behind you now, and those who have had enough can take the beautiful lakeside trail east to the *guardaparque* and the road back to Aluminé. (Incidentally, along this trail you will pass several spectacular waterfalls to bathe and recuperate under). Those made of sterner stuff will want to continue to the final lake, Moquehué, and will strike out stubbornly in the opposite direction, first west and then north, along the lakeside track by which the guards get their supplies of wine. The track fords two rivers. At the second, perhaps an hour and a half after leaving the *gendarmería*, you will find a convenient short cut to the Moquehué road. Just before the ford turn left to a corral. Here turn left again and follow the trail along the lefthand valley for a couple of hours until it peters out in a wide sloping pampa. Cut diagonally across it to a deserted ranch where you will find the road to Moquehué.

The road rises gently to 1450 metres, providing views of new snow capped peaks, some of them in Chile. Lago Moquehué comes into view which with its wooded island looks very like Derwentwater in the English Lake District. After six or seven hours you reach the village of Moquehué at the head of the lake. One more *gendarmería* post (no wine here) and you are free to sample the delights of the Hostería Bella Durmiente — hotel, restaurant and shop — with superb views of the lake. But first take the path to the right, 200 metres beyond the *hostería*, which leads down to the lake edge. Here dip a foot into the smooth, clear water. By doing so you will have completed one of the most difficult walks in the Argentine Lakes District.

Practical information

Time/rating You will need three to five days, or more if you want time to relax in those idyllic lakeside spots. The hiking is easy but finding your way is difficult in places. Allow plenty of time for going round in circles. The whole walk is about 80 kilometres. It is best done December to March.

Preparations Provisions can be bought in Zapala or Junín but tend to be limited and expensive. You can get any last minute odds and ends at the general store in Quillén. It is essential to take a compass.

Maps   Argentine IGM 1:100,000 Sheets 3972-29 (Quillén), 3972-23 (Lago Ñorquincó) and 3972-17 (Lago Aluminé) are adequate as long as you do not take them too literally. Crude regional maps are available free from the offices of the Dirección Provincial de Turismo in Zapala or Junín.

CERRO CHAPELCO
by John Pilkington

If you happen to be in San Martín de los Andes, do not miss the hike up to Cerro Chapelco. It is an easy four hour walk, so you could do the trip there and back in a day. Cerro Chapelco is Argentina's second biggest ski centre (after Cerro Catedral) with a restaurant, ski shop, chair lifts and ski tows as well as a *refugio* belonging to the local ski club (members only, but you may be able to talk your way in). The 15-kilometre trail climbs from 625 metres at San Martín to 1225 metres at the foot of the ski slopes, but those with a head for heights can take the chair lift to  Refugio Graeff at 1800 metres or Filo Chapelco at 1920 metres. From these points you will have a panoramic view of the *cordillera*, including the snow-capped Volcán Lanín to the north and Lago Lacar spread out far below. An even higher *refugio* is planned, at Filo Cerro, and if you choose you can walk higher still.

The trail starts at the south end of Calle Misionero Mascardi, five blocks east of the main *plaza* in San Martín. Climb straight up the hill and skirt the Hotel Sol de los Andes by the new paved road. The road forks 200 metres above the hotel, and a trail leads straight on from the junction nearest Chapelco. Zigzagging at first, it soon curves to the right and straightens out before meeting the road again at a sharp bend. From here you have a choice of walking up the road or following the variety of trails which run parallel to it. The trails are steeper but infinitely more pleasant. Take any which leaves the road to the right. You will find they all take you in the same direction, dividing and joining up again and intersecting the road at intervals as it winds its way up. For those who are not in a hurry, camping is possible all along the way, and the restaurant at the ski centre is surprisingly cheap.

LAGO LACAR THERMAL SPRINGS
by Rick Ansell

One of the best hot baths in Argentina! Take the daily excursion boat across Lago Lacar to Hua Hum, a pleasant crossing with a stop to visit a waterfall en route. From Hua Hum (*hosteria*) cross the exit river on the bridge and follow this dirt road up into the woods, past the *guadarparque*'s house. Ignore the several paths and tracks and after 20 minutes a road turns right marked 'Cascata' and 'Lago Queñi'. Take this road. It climbs very gently through the forest, past a farm. After a while it forks and the Cascata road goes to the left. Keep right and you will, almost without noticing, cross the pass and start to descend slightly. The road crosses a river on a wooden bridge and continues to Lago Queñi. About 2½ hours from Hua Hum you come to the *guardaparque*'s house where you can camp on the shore of the lake — perfect. For the spring, continue along the road for about 500m, when the road fords a wide, shallow river. Immediately afterwards a smaller track turns left marked 'Termas'. This path was the most beautiful forest path we followed, wide and clear and dry, through open forest and bamboo. 1½ hours will bring you to a steaming stream, crossing the path. The spring itself is about 100m uphill from the path. You can camp beside the main path here, which continues south. We returned the way we had come.

RÍO BUENO TO VALDIVIA
by Nick Cotton

This beautiful five day walk along totally unspoilt Pacific coastline combines vast sandy beaches with magical forests perched above the sea and has the added bonus of including interesting boat trips each end. It is probably best to do the hike south to north so as to be sure of getting transport as there is only one boat a week to the southern end. However, we have received reports that some people have had difficulties and that the boat service at the start of this walk no longer runs. Make enquiries before setting out. We  would appreciate any information on whether there are any alternative boat services. Best time to go is November to March.

Getting there

You start from La Unión, a one and a half hour bus ride from Valdivia or Osorno. From here walk, hitch or share a taxi to Trumao, a small settlement on the Río Bueno six kilometres to the southwest. (There is no bus service). From Trumao, there used to be a steam boat service on Saturday to the mouth of Río Bueno, a breathtaking, six-hour trip through the mountains. Enquire at the travel agency in the main square in La Unión next to the Hotel Turismo. If you are unable to get a boat to the mouth of Río Bueno, consider shortening the walk and starting at Hueicolla.

Directions

Ask the boat captain to drop you at Venecia, a one-house settlement on the north bank of the river just before it reaches the sea. If, however, the boat will only stop at La Barra on the south bank, you will have to pay someone to row you across. There are no fixed prices for the river crossings so it is best to negotiate a price before starting a trip.

From Venecia climb the dirt road which leads north towards Hueicolla. You can walk straight to Hueicolla but it is worth taking a diversion to the tiny fishing settlement of Lameguapi.

After about 40 minutes turn off left down a sandy path which leads through the forest and reaches Lameguapi after two hours. Half way along the beach at Lameguapi follow the stream which climbs the hillside and joins a path going north. Follow this for about one and a half hours and after a steep climb you will rejoin the Venecia/Hueicolla dirt road. It is then a two hour downhill walk to Hueicolla, a small coastal village of about 30 holiday houses, where you can celebrate with a fine seafood meal at the *hostería*.

At the point where the road to La Unión turns sharply east at the end of Hueicolla Bay, walk straight on until you reach a small river. Again you will have to find a boat to take you across. Continue for two hours along the beach until it ends then follow the well-worn path which climbs steeply through the forest over Punta Colún. When you come down to the Río Colún on the other side, walk upstream for half a mile then shout and whistle for a rowing boat. A wonderful *señora* in a most interesting hat rowed us across. Follow the river back along the north bank towards the sea and walk along the next beach past huge sand dunes and cows chewing on seaweed.

Two hours from Río Colún, a path at the end of the beach takes you over another promontory, Punta Galera. After another one and a half hour's up-and-down walking you reach the fishing village of Punta Galera where there is good camping beyond the houses.

From here the path stays well above the sea, winding through forest until it reaches the Río Chaihuín. There was a proper bridge across this until some dim timber merchant took his heavily laden juggernaut across. Having been built only to take oxcarts, horses and light vehicles, it collapsed. You can still walk across the remains, however. At Chaihuín there is a small store where you can get basic food.

From here there are two alternative ways of getting to the village of Corral. You can either take the road, which is fairly boring but faster (about seven hours). Or you can walk to the end of the bay and pick up the coastal path which takes about nine hours to Corral. If you take the road route you will need to stock up on water beforehand as the first stream is not until three hours after Chaihuín. From Corral there are about five boats a day to Niebla and Valdivia.

NOTE: Paradoxically, despite the region's high rainfall, water is a problem so always fill your bottle whenever you come to a stream. It is probably best to camp on or near the beach where there are streams as there is very little surface water on the sandy, well drained hills above the sea.

Practical information
Distance/time   Five days at average speed, including the boat trips and river crossings.

Preparations   You will need camping equipment, waterproofs, waterbottles, small change to pay for rowing boats. You should take food for four to five days, although you can find basics in Hueicolla and at Chaihuín.

PUERTO VARAS TO PUERTO MONTT
by John Pilkington

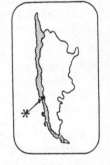

For a nice day's stroll through the gently rolling lowlands of southern Chile before you get involved with the tougher stuff on some of the other hikes, take the old road which winds for 22 kilometres between Puerto Varas and Puerto Montt. The trip is best done from north to south, which will allow you to face away from the sun and to pick up a local bus from Alerce, halfway to Puerto Montt, if you feel the urge.

From the Plaza de Armas in Puerto Varas follow the lakeside road east for a kilometre to Puerto Chico. The cone of Volcán Osorno is visible in the east, as indeed it is for the whole hike. At Puerto Chico a road to the right, signposted to Alerce, will lead you for ten kilometres through intensive dairy farming country interspersed with orchards. (*Clare adds*: We have had one report that the signpost no longer exists, in which case you should seek local advice). Near Alerce the scene becomes very English, with high banks and hedgerows on either side. Alerce itself has a single main street, a few shops and a railway station, but little else to distinguish it since much of its population works in Puerto Montt. From here on you become

THE ISLAND OF CHILOÉ

Only a narrow stretch of water separates Chiloé from the Chilean mainland, but crossing it is like stepping into another country. The island, 250 kilometres long by 50 kilometres wide, in many ways resembles an island in the Scottish Hebrides: much of the time it is shrouded in rain and mist, but when the sun shines it is extremely beautiful. Around the coast is an emerald and gold patchwork of potato and wheat fields and the island's two main towns, Ancud and Castro. In the interior are vast virgin forests.

Chiloé's 116,000 tough, dark skinned inhabitants are the mixed descendants of the Mapuche from the Temuco region, and the Chonos from the islands of Aisén, to the south. Most live off fishing (look out for the local sailing sloops, or *lanchas*). Seaweed is harvested for export to Japan. Handicrafts are also important: many of the plain, undyed woollen products you see for sale in Puerto Montt are made on the island. You can also buy them in Chiloé.

The island is perhaps best known for its quaint wooden houses, or *palafitos*, built over the water on stilts so that boats can be moored underneath when the tide comes in. These can be seen at Ancud, Castro, Quemchi and Chonchi. The island also has about 150 beautiful wooden churches, built by the Jesuits who settled here in the 17th and 18th centuries. The oldest were built without the use of a single iron nail. Dating from the same period is the tradition of using wooden tiles on the walls and roofs of houses. If you look closely, you will find about a dozen different shapes and styles of tiles. In Ancud you can see one of the forts which the Spanish, who had seized Chiloé in 1567, used to defend themselves in the War of Independence. The island was the Spaniards' last Chilean stronghold and they were not defeated until 1826.

Patrick Symington writes: "We visited the National Park of Chiloé, which is on the wild Pacific coast. It doesn't rain quite so much over this side. To get there go first to Castro or Chouchi and then take the local bus to Cucao. This is a charming little place which features in a short story by Bruce Chatwin in his collection *What Am I Doing Here?* From here it is a half-hour walk to the Park Visitor Centre and campsite. We didn't trek any further, but I believe you can walk for miles up the coast. The campsite is in an attractive setting, and there are interesting day walks in the woods and out onto the beach to see the great Pacific rolling in. There are sand-dunes, too. Food is available in the village. The whole trip makes a very nice change from the mountain walking and scenery of the rest of Chile.

There are three main ways of getting to Chiloé from the mainland. The first is the Cruz del Sur ferry which operates between Chacao at the northern tip of the island, and Pargua across the straits on the mainland. Or you can take one of the Transmarchilay Ltda ferries which operate between Quellón, in southern Chiloé, and Puerto Chacabuco; and between Chonchi, central Chiloé, and Chaitén. Transmarchilay has offices at Libertad 669, Ancud (tel 2317); 21 de Mayo 417, Coyhaique (tel 23 1971); Av. Costanera, Quellón (tel 319); Corcovado 266 (tel 272); Angelmó 1666, Puerto Montt (tel 25 4654)."

increasingly aware of the city ahead as first its airfield and then its outer suburbs come into view. You approach it through a rather temporary looking housing estate and then, turning left where a sign says 'Plaza 2 km', find yourself on the edge of an escarpment with the city spread out below. Ten minutes down Calle Ejército and you will be in the Plaza de Armas by Reloncaví Sound, enjoying an ice cold beer or a soothing mug of hot chocolate. Alternatively, you may decide to catch a bus from Alerce to Puerto Montt as the first part of the walk (as far as Alerce) is undoubtedly the best.

VOLCÁN OSORNO
by John Pilkington

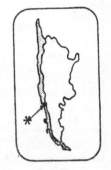

Another easy day's walk, with stupendous views near the top, is from Ensenada, on the road to Petrohué and Ralún, to the two *refugios* on Volcán Osorno. Refugio Los Pumas, 12 kilometres from Ensenada, is 900 metres up the 2720 metre volcano, while the Teski Club one at 15 kilometres is 300 metres higher. You can eat and sleep quite cheaply at both. Los Pumas is open all the year round and for us was the cosier of the two.

The ascent to the summit has recently gained a reputation for being dangerous, mainly because inexperienced climbers have attempted it in poor weather conditions and killed themselves by falling into crevasses. But if you are properly equipped (ice-axe, crampons, rope, etc) this is a magnificent climb. If you wish to do it, we recommend you enquire at the tourist office in Puerto Montt for details of the agencies which organize trips to the summit, such as La Babuja (see next page).

Getting to Ensenada is easy. You can hitchhike or take one of the Transportes Esmeralda buses from Avenida Diego Portales bus station in Puerto Montt. From Ensenada take the road signposted Yerbas Buenas for two kilometres until you come to the junction with the road to the *refugios*. On the way you will pass Laguna Verde, a tiny emerald lake in a clearing from where you can gaze over the vast expanse of the Lago Llanquihue. Soon you will find yourself climbing past meadows and small farms where fruit and honey can be bought.

The vegetation on these lower slopes is bewildering in its variety. You will find birch, bamboo, bilberry and blackberry bushes and the *chilco* plant with its delicate red bell-shaped flowers, among lots of others. As you climb, the vegetation thins out and you glimpse the lake. The ascent is steady and gradual on a clear gravel track all the way, and if you get bored with the views you can test your walking speed against the kilometre posts which have been thoughtfully put in.

P. Frew writes: "Do not dream of climbing Osorno alone or without proper gear. From the hut the mountain, like all volcanoes, appears very foreshortened: when you reach the top of the ski lift you are only half way to the edge of the glacier. There are enormous crevasses as soon as you are on the ice so you *must* be roped up. The route is fairly obvious, to the left of a bare, rocky area, then directly up, negotiating the crevasses. Timing: two hours to the glacier, three more hours to the summit. You should leave at dawn. With fine weather the view from the summit over Lago Todos los Santos to Tronador and Puntiagudo is superb. There is no crater — the summit is a flat plateau. It is worth visiting some ice caves on the northern side of the summit, where the ice has melted so you can walk underneath it. Do not stray too near the edge to the east as there are dangerous crevasses."

If you like 'oldy worldy' things or feel like a good bath, the Hotel Ensenada is well worth visiting on your way to or from Volcán Osorno. The hotel, run by German immigrants since the turn of the century, is built in typical Nordic style and has a fantastic collection of antiques and bizarre memorabilia ranging from fire extinguishers to a polyphon which plays the Chilean national anthem. It also has an old fashioned swimming pool, which looks like a Roman bath and whose waters are a murky green. The hotel's apple *Kuchen* (cake) is ... well, out of this world.

La Barbuja ski resort is now open all year ($25 with breakfast) and runs climbing trips up Osorno. The complete package with guide and equipment costs $50 per person. Information from the Hotel Vicente Perez Rosales in Puerto Montt.

Practical information
Time/rating An easy four hour walk to the hut, well marked all the way. To the summit a strenuous five hours.

Preparation You can stay and buy food at both *refugios*, but check with the Hotel Ensenada that they are open. Temperatures can be low at night, so a warm sleeping bag is essential.

Map Chilean IGM 1:50,000 Sheet 4100-7230 (Las Cascadas).

FROM THE COAST TO LAKE TODOS LOS SANTOS
by John Pilkington

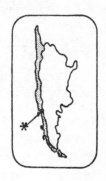

This short walk was described in the first edition as 'one of the most breathtakingly beautiful we can remember' but the building of a road to Cochamó and the difficulty of crossing lake Todos los Santos to make it a round trip has made it less rewarding in recent years. It is still a lovely walk, however, and simple to follow. The main part from Ralún to Cayutué can easily be done in a day, but it can be stretched out in a couple of delightful ways, either by starting at Cochamó and walking along the estuary to Ralún, or by striking east from Lago Cayutué for a few days to explore the valley of the Río Blanco. On most of the trails you will pass through lush lowland pastures, forests of giant birches and *arrayanes* (these are the trees with the strange reddish peeling bark) and masses of blackberry, bilberry and blueberry bushes. You will see not only the tidal Estuaria Reloncaví and Lago Todos los Santos — known too as Lago Esmeralda because of its brilliant bluish-green hue — but also the remote and enchanting Lago Cayutué surrounded by thickly forested mountains. The farms you will pass have milk, cheese and sometimes honey for sale to fend off any pangs of hunger left unsatisfied by the trailside fruits.

Getting there

By far the nicest way of reaching the trail is to take a boat: either from Puerto Montt to one of the villages on the Reloncaví estuary, or across Lago Todos los Santos. We've described the walk from south to north — i.e. starting from the estuary — but the uncertainty of transport at the lake end (see below) has led many of our readers to do it the other way round. In Petrohué, with persistence, you'll usually be able to find a small boat to take you to the northern starting point at Cayutué. This two-hour crossing should cost between \$18 and \$30 per person.

Since the opening of the road from Puerto Varas, boats from Puerto Montt no longer serve the southern starting points of Cochamó and Ralún. However, we've had reports of a twice-weekly service to Puelo or Sotomó, tiny hamlets on the Reloncaví estuary about 25 kilometres south of Cochamó. For the latest information on this, ask at the tourist office in Puerto Montt. The road from Cochamó will eventually be extended along the estuary to join the

Carretera Austral. Until this happens, the only sure way to reach Ralún and Cochamó will be by the Transportes Esmeralda buses which leave Puerto Montt daily except Sundays, calling at Puerto Varas.

If you walk the route from north to south, try to finish at the main road by 3.30pm for the onward bus to Cochamó, or by 6.00pm for the service to Puerto Varas and Puerto Montt. (There's also an early morning bus to Puerto Montt, leaving Cochamó about 8.00am.)

Directions

Cochamó is pure delight: a quaint fishing village with a few restaurants and shops, although not quite as peaceful as it was before the road was built to Ralún a few years ago. The Hotel Cochamó has been highly recommended. From here you can walk or take the bus to Ralún, on the other side of the beautiful Reloncaví estuary. This is just a string of houses, including the exclusive Hotel Ralún (boats and even aeroplanes for hire!) There is also a nice tin shack restaurant called El Refugio where you can get a simple meal of delicious fish and tomato salad.

The trail to Lago Todos los Santos starts on the Cochamó side of the Río Petrohué at the head of the estuary and turns north intially along a dusty new road) towards Lago Cayutué. It's clear all the way — a comfortable day's walk which will take you over a low (480 metre) pass.

After about six hours you will reach the junction with the Río Blanco trail (see below) and almost immediately find yourself on the shores of Lago Cayutué. Fallen trees sometimes block the path here. A further three hours' easy walking will bring you to Lago Todos los Santos where the trail ends at a small ranch. There are some beautiful camping spots on the lake shore.

On weekdays a farmer called Ramón Saez offers lodging and onward transport in his small boat to Petrohué, which lies under the towering, snow-capped peak of Volcán Osorno. He leaves early in the morning, so you should arrive at Petrohué in time to catch the 9.00am ferry to Peulla and the start of the international hike (see page 119). Alternatively you can return to Puerto Varas or Puerto Montt, or explore the volcano (see page 115).

Jim Lunsford adds: There is an interesting side trip from this hike into the valley of the Río Blanco. Just before Lago Cayutué turn right and follow the trail over a low pass for about 15 kilometres to the Río Blanco. This is a remote and beautiful valley with just a few small farms. The farmers occasionally make boat trips across Lago

Todos los Santos from Vuriloche to Peulla, and you may be lucky enough to be offered a lift. Otherwise you must return the way you came. Alternatively, Patrick Symington suggests starting the walk in Petrohué, where he was able to hire a boat to take two for $25. [We would appreciate your comments on the recent state of this trail.]

Practical information
Time/rating It takes about a day to reach Lago Todos los Santos from Ralún, longer if you camp en route. If you want to explore the Río Blanco valley, you will need several days. None of the hiking is difficult but in the Río Blanco valley the trails may be indistinct.

Preparations You can buy much of your food at the farms along the way, but bread can only be bought in Cochamó or from private houses in Ralún. It is probably best, though, to get bread and substantial provisions in Puerto Varas or Puerto Montt. In the Río Blanco valley there are only a few small farms so you will need your own supplies.

Maps Chilean IGM 1:50,000 Sheets 4115-7215 (Cochamó) and 4100-7215 (Petrohué) will cover you for the main hike (the latter is optional). You will need Sheets 4115-7200 (Río Cochamó) and 4100-7200 (Peulla) for the Río Blanco side trip.

AN INTERNATIONAL HIKE:
LAKE TODOS LOS SANTOS TO LAKE MASCARDI
by John Pilkington, Clare Hargreaves and John and Christine Myerscough, updated by Sebastian Cooper and Elizabeth Allison

Some of the most spectacular mountain and glacier scenery in South America lies on the Chile/Argentina border, between Puerto Montt and Bariloche. Most people travelling the 200 kilometres between these towns end up taking one of the high priced tours ($60 or more) which afford little time to absorb the

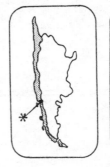

remarkable landscape en route. By hiking and hitchhiking you can cover the route for about a fifth of this price, the only unavoidable

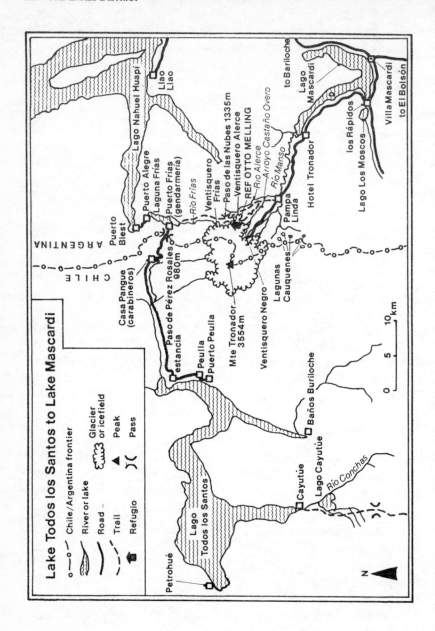

Lake Todos los Santos to Lake Mascardi

cost being the boat across Lago Todos los Santos which is about $20, and enjoy the mountains, lakes and glaciers first hand.

The core of the trip is the walk from Peulla on Lago Todos los Santos in Chile to Pampa Linda in the valley of the Río Manso in Argentina, a distance of 50 kilometres or three to four days' strenuous walking. The remainder, apart from the boat trip, can be walked, bussed or hitchhiked according to how you feel. We found the frontier officials very helpful and not at all put out by some scruffy *mochileros* wanting to enter their country. If entering Argentina from Chile you will have to eat up all your provisions of fresh food beforehand as fruits, fresh meat, cheese and other dairy products cannot to taken across the border. Note also that changing currency can be a problem (although the hotel at Peulla does change dollar travellers cheques if you are walking east to west) so be sure to carry a small quantity of each currency before doing the trip.

Rick Ansell writes that it is possible to link this walk up with the Lake to Lake walk on the Argentine side (see page 137). Evidently, the hotel will ferry people across Lago Mascardi for a few dollars or, alternatively, there is a path to the west of the lake with a bridge which crosses Río Manso.

Getting there

An alternative to hitchhiking between Puerto Varas and Petrohué on the northern end of Lago Todos los Santos is to take the local bus which goes daily to Petrohué via Ensenada. (Times keep changing so you will have to check in Puerto Varas). The boat across Lago Todos los Santos leaves Petrohué Monday to Friday at 9.00am, returning from Peulla at 3.00pm. The trip takes about two hours. In summer, however, there are often extra boats so it is worth asking at travel agencies in Puerto Montt, Puerto Varas or Bariloche the day before you leave. On the Argentine side, the Mercedes bus company runs between Villa Mascardi and Bariloche or El Bolsón. The bus from Bariloche leaves at 9.00am Monday, Wednesday and Friday, passing Villa Mascardi about an hour later before continuing to El Bolsón. The return bus leaves El Bolsón at 2.00pm Tuesday, Thursday and Saturday, passing Villa Mascardi around 4.00pm. A bus leaves Pampa Linda for Bariloche at 4.30 pm in summer.

Don't start the walk on a Sunday: the immigration office at Peulla is closed, and there are no regular boats across Lago Todos los Santos.

Directions

We walked from west to east, that is, from Chile to Argentina and have described the hike this way. It can be done equally well the other way round, but if doing this you should read the note at the end of this section.

The walk begins on the jetty at Peulla where you will disembark around 11.00am from the boat which brought you across Lago Todos los Santos. The village itself is a kilometre down the road, and consists of about a dozen houses, a post office, a camp site and the expensive Hotel Peulla. No shops, but you may be able to buy fresh bread at the hotel or at one of the houses. You will also find the Chilean customs and international police here. You must call on both before you leave the country.

The dirt road over the Paso de Pérez Rosales to Argentina lets you in gently for the first 18 kilometres by keeping to the wide, flat valley floor. You will pass a large *estancia* then, after about four hours, cross Río Peulla. Half an hour on and you will arrive at the Chilean *carabineros* at Casa Pangue in an idyllic setting with views of glacier-capped Mount Tronador to the south. The incumbents of this isolated post are a friendly bunch, and will probably let you pitch your tent around here if it is getting late. Otherwise, it is another four hours over the pass to Argentina and Puerto Frías. From Casa Pangue the road climbs steeply uphill as if forever (about seven kilometres). There is a *refugio* about half a kilometre before the pass where you can stop if it all gets too much. The pass is densely forested and only once do you get a really good view of the river far below. But once over the top and into Argentina it is a mere hour (four kilometres) down to the Argentine customs and *gendarmería* at Puerto Frías.

Some people prefer to skip this part of the walk, however, and pick up one of the tour buses which go from Peulla to Puerto Frías in the mornings. This may be quite expensive but if you do not fancy walking it is the only option as there is no car traffic on this road.

Laguna Frías, from which the port takes its name, is a magical place. Cradled between high forest-covered mountains, its silent waters are an astonishing emerald green; (but beware: the minerals that give the lake this romantic look will give you a stomach ache too). The policemen at the *gendarmería* are very friendly, being only too pleased to have someone to talk to in their lonely post. They will point you to good camping spots in the woods where you can feast on wild raspberries if you are there in summer.

The hike continues along a trail which winds left through the woods just above the *gendarmería* towards the aptly named Paso de las Nubes — Pass of the Clouds. Ask the policemen if you are in any doubt as to where the path begins. It is clear and wide at first, but after the first hour or so narrows into an obstacle course of overhanging bamboo and fallen tree trunks. From time to time the *guardaparque* of Nahuel Huapí National Park clear these away and restore the waymarks which consist of white plastic strips tied to branches and paint flashes on trees and rocks.

Not far from Puerto Frías you will pass a small monument dedicated to '*Commander Julio Cesar Sagredo and Deputy Commander Pedro Angel Obregón, who fell in this place on 13th April 1952 in the fulfilment of their duty*' (the two unfortunate men died when their aeroplane crashed here). You will soon come to the Río Frías, which you should follow along the river bank for about 30 minutes until you reach the spot where a huge tree has fallen across the river forming a natural bridge. (Be very careful crossing this after heavy rain when it will be partially submerged and dangerous. Also take care not to overshoot this tree trunk bridge as the path still takes you to where the old suspension bridge used to be a few yards further on.) You will reach a small but good camp site on the trail about 15 minutes later. This is the only camp site between Puerto Frías and Ventisquero Frías.

The next three or four hours are spent scrambling over tree trunks through a thick forest of bamboo and *arrayán*. Keep your eyes skinned for plastic or paper strips tied to branches which indicate the way. You eventually emerge at a quite remarkable spot. Directly across the valley, a glacier tumbles down from Mount Tronador in a mass of blue ice, crevasses and glacier-borne gravel (though this has retreated dramatically in recent years); ahead the valley ends in a sheer wall of rock; and below, just across some small rocky outcrops there is a beautiful camp site among the trees beside a stream. The only thing likely to bother you as you listen to the distant thud of falling avalanches are the horseflies (*tábanos* in Spanish) which at certain times of year get extremely fat and troublesome.

When continuing be careful not to lose the path — fighting your way through the bush is well nigh impossible. After crossing the stream just beyond the camp site, the path almost immediately starts climbing up the bare rock outcrop to your left as you look at the glacier. When the path peters out, head uphill towards the forest and skirt its edge until you find a path heading up into the forest near a white arrow painted on the flat rock. If you reach a stream running down from the forest to the valley, you have gone too far. The path is marked with red paint on trees and is fairly clear. After five minutes you reach a stream which you must wade or jump across. The path is clearly visible on the other side. It climbs steeply for about an hour and a half until you reach the 1335-metre pass in an area of thorn bushes. Incredible views, *nubes* permitting, in all directions but especially to the north where Laguna Frías can be seen in its hollow among the soaring peaks. If you do the walk in December or early January you are warned that there is likely to be snow on the pass which makes walking tough, and finding your way difficult. Remember the path descends in zig-zags. Just below the summit there are lush meadows where you can camp or there is a place by the Río Alerce, just across the swampy area (see below).

The trail winds down through the forest again and after about two hours (slow, because of the many fallen trees across the path) you will come to a swamp where it all but disappears. Keep your eyes peeled for the white plastic markers. Do not head towards the river but go straight into the swamp for about 50 metres until you come across a line of submerged logs heading slightly to the right. The next plastic marker is visible from these logs in a tree 30 metres ahead. From there the trail becomes clearer again if somewhat boggy, keeping to the right bank of the river. The forested landscape gets better all the time and you can camp almost anywhere.

After about two hours you meet the trail from Refugio Otto Melling (see below) and cross over the Arroyo Castaño Overo when you see a grassy camp site on the other side of the river with a wooden sign. There used to be a bridge, but it is now completely dilapidated and you will have to wade over the river instead, or try crossing on fallen trees. The going is easy for the final 30 minutes to Pampa Linda where you enjoy spectacular views of Mount Tronador, not to mention the material delights of the *hostería* ($54 for a room for two with breakfast and a huge, four-course dinner for $12), shop and fully equipped camp site (even hot showers in season). Here too you can get information from the *guardaparque* about hikes to other places, such as Ventisquero Negro (four hours), Lagunas Cauquenes (five hours) and Refugio Otto Melling (six hours).

If you have time it is worth going up to Refugio Otto Melling. "You will see the hut signposted after fording the river above Pampa Linda. It is two hours through the forest to the treeline (a steep footpath cuts off the curves of the jeep track) and above the trees are spectacular views of the glaciers and waterfalls. A further hour brings you to the *refugio* which is positioned on a rock ridge with glaciers on both sides and condors flying around it. The guardian will guide groups of climbers up Tronador to Pico Argentino and to Pico Internacional." (P.Frew)

From Pampa Linda a tourist road winds for about 40 kilometres down to Villa Mascardi, on the paved road from Bariloche to El Bolsón. We would not blame you if you thumbed a lift as the walk can be tedious and there is quite a bit of traffic. After 4.00pm you can usually get a lift in a tour bus returning to Bariloche. They will charge about $10. If you do hitch, however, bear in mind that the road to Pampa Linda is one way — up in the morning and down after 2.00pm — so if no traffic seems to be going your way that might be why. If you want to camp, there are only two viable places because the lakeside is steep and heavily forested: on the beach at the head of Lago Mascardi just before the youth camp; or at the Los Rápidos camp site 12 kilometres further on.

From Los Rápidos (zero point for the roadside kilometre posts) you can take a road down to Lago Hess and the other lakes in the lower valley of the Río Manso. Otherwise it is nine kilometres through pleasant rolling countryside to the main road to Bariloche.

NOTE: If you do the walk east to west you should note the following points. As you leave Pampa Linda the trail forks. Take the left fork. After crossing the bridge follow the jeep road up the hill, ignoring signs that tell you otherwise. If you lose the trail, look for a large cairn with white paint markings which indicates where the path branches off the track.

Make sure you have some Chilean money to pay for the boat from Peulla to Petrohué.

Practical information

Distance/time From Peulla to Lago Mascardi is about four days, but the hike can be shortened by up to a day at either end if you take transport. It can also be combined with the *Lake to lake* walk near Bariloche, to make a longer hike. The going is sometimes difficult in places because of fallen trees and the trail may be hard to follow. The immigration authorities on both sides of the border are closed on Sundays.

Preparations Stock up with food in Puerto Montt or Puerto Varas (or Bariloche or El Bolsón if you are doing it the other way). There are very few supplies *en route* — other than the luscious blackberries, raspberries and strawberries which you will find all along the hike.

Maps Argentine IGM 1:100,000 Sheet 4172-22 (Llao-Llao) covers the most important part of this hike, but the latest edition we could find was not very accurate. Not surprising, really: it was published in 1947. If you are walking east to west you should visit the Club Andino in Bariloche as their free booklet of hikes covers most of this walk and is very helpful.

THE CERRO CATEDRAL CIRCUIT
by John Pilkington

Although mostly little higher than 2000 metres, the peaks of the Catedral range must be among the most rugged in South America. You might expect an excursion to such an area to take a matter of weeks, but this circuit can be done in just three days, starting and finishing in Bariloche. The shorter circuit can be done in a single day.

Much of the landscape is rough and rocky but nowhere are the trails dangerous. They have been excellently waymarked by the Club Andino Bariloche, whose *refugios* provide shelter and make a nice change from camping. Part of the walk covers the same area as the Hut to Hut walk (page 131).

The trails are passable from November to April, but at the beginning and end of the season the *refugios* may be closed. Check at the Club's headquarters before you leave (see *Preparations*).

Getting there
The directions which follow begin at the foot of the Catedral range at a cross known as La Virgen de las Nieves (Virgin of the Snows). However, if you can, try to go straight to the ski village, ten kilometres further along the road towards Cerro Catedral. During the high summer and winter seasons the Mercedes bus company runs buses direct to the ski village, but the service is variable. To find out if the buses are running, ask at the Direccíon Municipal de Turismo in the Centro Cívico in Bariloche.

Directions
See page 132 for map.
Buses leave for the Virgen every half hour from the shelter at the corner of Calles Moreno and Rolando in Bariloche. They are marked Teleférico/Virgen de las Nieves and the 20 minute journey gives you a good view of Bariloche's opulent western suburbs overlooking Lago Nahuel Huapí.

The Virgin herself is rather disappointing so you will probably want to head straight up the wide paved road towards Cerro Catedral. Somewhere on this 10-kilometre stretch you are almost certain to be offered a lift to the giant car park built to serve the skier freaks who come here in their droves in winter. However, the walk up the road is a nice one, with the rocky Catedral Norte looming up ahead, and the gradual climb lets you in gently for the stiffer stuff later. If you do walk this stretch, leave the paved road when you see the buildings of the ski village, about an hour's walk from the Virgin. By following a trail to the left of two electricity lines you will come to the old road to the village and cut two or three kilometres off your walk.

However you get to the ski village, you will want to take time to wander round before charging off up the mountain. Set in a natural bowl, the ski schools, equipment shops, *hosterías, confiterías* and hotel are housed in an assortment of neo-Tyrolean buildings reminiscent of a Hollywood film set.

More decisions have to be taken here. You can reach the first main *refugio*, Refugio Frey by two routes: one begins at Refugio Lynch near the top of the cable car and approaches Refugio Frey from above; the other leads south from the ski village car park and takes around four hours. We chose the first, having been told about its spectacular views. After some of the wildest backpacking we have ever done we discovered just what an understatement this was. However we came back later to try the alternative route, and found this good in its own way too. We have described it on page 129.

To reach the beginning of the first route you can ride up in style by cable car and chair lift, or walk up. Tough nuts who decide to walk should take the trail underneath the Piedra del Condor chair lift, and after about half an hour up the second stage of the chair lift follow the vehicle track which bears off to the left. Total climbing time three to four hours. Refugio Lynch offers breathtaking views of Lago Nahuel Huapí — not to mention tea, coffee and fizzy drinks.

The trail to Refugio Frey starts from the little peak just beyond the meteorological station. It is well marked with yellow, and later red, paint, and although you will scarcely believe the terrain you have just crossed, you will be in no danger of getting lost. The path reaches its highest point at Punta Nevada (2090 metres), then drops down to a saddle between two fierce looking rocky outcrops. The next one or two hours are spent negotiating an incredible traverse at about 2000 metres, with rocky needles towering directly above and very little for 500 metres below. Vertigo sufferers beware!

Finally, after meeting the trail from Refugio Jakob which you will be taking the next day, the path slices through a narrow canyon in the watershed and drops down steeply beneath snowfields to the tiny Laguna Schmoll. If you do the walk in spring or early summer you will almost certainly have to cross snow, so it is essential to take an ice-axe and to know how to use it.

After passing over the lip of the perfectly formed corrie containing Laguna Schmoll, the trail drops down sharply again to the softer shores of Laguna Tonček. At the far end of this tiny lake is a little grey house with a bright red roof called Refugio Frey (see Hut to Hut walk, page 131). It does not exactly have all mod cons, but is a welcome sight in such lunar country.

You can return direct to the ski village from here by the alternative route, in which case you will be back at the car park in about three hours. In fact this shorter circuit, which can be done in a day if you use the cable car, is a good way of seeing Cerro Catedral if you do not fancy the longer hike or are pressed for time. Follow a clear wide trail which is steep at first but rapidly eases off into a pleasant woodland walk. A little over half an hour from Refugio Frey you will pass the fairytale Refugio Petricek or Piedrita (little rock), a tiny cabin ingeniously built round a giant overhanging boulder. Another half hour and you will come to a fork: the path to the right leads down to the trail around Lago Gutiérrez; the one to the left contours the hillside back to the ski village. Towards the end the trail divides once or twice, but all paths lead eventually to the village car park.

Those who have plumped for the longer circuit should head up the valley from Refugio Frey to the junction at the watershed. If you came down from this junction the previous day you will know the way. If not, keep to the right of the first lake (Laguna Tonček) and where the valley ends climb up along the stream which drops down from the right. This will bring you to the second lake, Laguna Schmoll. By passing to the left of this you will be able to climb up to the cleft in the watershed which brings you to the junction. The path from Refugio Frey to this point is marked by yellow and red paint and will take between one and two hours.

At the junction a big red arrow marked Ref. Jacob points over the edge of a 500-metre drop. Many have flunked the hike at this sight, but it is really not as bad as it looks. Take the big rocks slowly, then slither down the scree any way you like. The route is well marked throughout (red paint this time). When you reach the meadow in the valley bottom, after perhaps an hour of glissading down the mountain, keep to the lefthand side by the trees. The path soon enters the trees, well marked by red paint. After the far end, after washing off the sweat in a crystal clear stream (the last water before Refugio Jakob) you will be ready for the one or two hour climb to the second watershed.

Unlike the first, this ridge is in full view all the way up, and gives the disconcerting impression of receding as you climb. If you find this too depressing, look behind you at the pinnacles and flanking buttresses of 2409-metre Cerro Catedral rising steadily above the western horizon as you ascend. An awe-inspiring sight. Your own summit, at about 1850 metres, is rather lower than this but just as dizzy. Ahead the valley of Arroyo Casa de Piedra is spread out beneath you, and at its head Laguna Jakob nestling beneath a low pass. The *refugio* occupies an idyllic spot on a rocky outcrop overlooking the lake. English hearts will be especially gladdened by the sanitary arrangements, in a little hut called Winchester Cathedral.

From Refugio Jakob it is possible to walk to the Club Andino's two other *refugios* in the area, Segre and López, although the route is tough and unwaymarked for the first section. This is described in the Hut to Hut walk. The route is waymarked from Refugio Jakob as far as Laguna Los Témpanos, an easy 45 minute walk over ice-polished rock, and this makes a nice morning's stroll if you are heading back down the valley. The lake is cold and eerie with permanent snow right down to the water's edge.

The trail down the valley of Arroyo Casa de Piedra is well trodden by feet and hooves. Apart from a short rocky stretch negotiated by an iron ladder it is mostly gently downhill and you can be at the main road in five hours. Near the bottom are some idyllic picnic or camping spots for those not in a hurry: soft grassy banks beside clear blue-green waters in a wooded valley-within-a-valley. For those anxious to return to the more sophisticated delights of Bariloche, turn right at the main road and you will eventually reach a place called Puerto Moreno where you can pick up the half-hourly Mercedes bus from Llao-Llao.

The alternative route to Refugio Frey

This gentler introduction to the Cerro Catedral massif takes you through heath and woodland across the lower slopes of the mountain but still high above Lago Gutiérrez over which you will have spectacular views. When you reach the ski village car park, look for an isolated pair of white houses on the far side. They are reached by a track from the main road 200 metres from the car park entrance, and the trail starts behind them — or rather, several trails start, but they soon join into one. It is well marked all the way to Refugio Frey. After two hours you will meet the trail coming up from Lago Gutiérrez and turn northwest along Arroyo van Titter. This is crossed a little further on by a precarious footbridge and then, quite suddenly, you come across Refugio Piedrita nestling under its huge boulder. This remarkable little place was built in 1978 by the Club Andino Esloveno, the climbing club of the Yugoslav community in Argentina, to replace the previous one destroyed by fire. The ethnic influence is evident in the beautifully painted designs on the window shutters, as well as in the names of the nearby lakes. However, the *refugio* is kept locked, so brace yourself and push on. In another hour you will be sipping hot *mate* in Refugio Frey.

Practical information
Time/rating   Refugio Lynch via Refugio Frey to Villa Catedral, one day. Villa Catedral via Refugios Lynch, Frey and Jakob to Puerto Moreno, three days. The hike includes some scree scrambling but the trails are all well marked.

Preparations   A visit to the Club Andino Bariloche is a must for this hike. They will tell you not only about trail and weather conditions, but also whether the *refugios* are open. If you intend to try the very long hike to Refugios Segre and López it is essential to tell them your intended route and to get the very fullest directions. You will find the Club at Calle 20 de Febrero 30, at the corner of Calle Morales, just behind the national park administration building.

Buy all your food in Bariloche before you leave. The ski village at Cerro Catedral has plenty of restaurants but no shops, and the *refugios* carry food only for emergencies. An ice-axe is essential if you are doing the walk in spring or early summer before the lower snowfields have melted.

Maps   For want of anything better we suggest you look at Argentina IGM 1:100,000 Sheets 4172-23 (Bariloche) and 4172-22 (Llao-Llao). But unless you can lay your hands on editions more recent than 1947, do not bother actually buying them. The Club Andino Bariloche may be able to help.

HUT TO HUT WALK IN THE BARILOCHE AREA
by Christine and John Myerscough

This challenging four to five day circuit takes you through some of
the country's wildest and most dramatic scenery via four of the Club
Andino's comfortable *refugios*. This allows you to leave your tent
behind and to travel light. If, however, you want to camp there are
plenty of good spots. Many sections are tough going and from
Refugio Jakob to Refugio Segre the route is not waymarked. The
walk, which includes a large amount of scrambling up and down
steep scree and boulders, is not recommended for beginners.

Getting there
The walk starts from the northern end of Lago Gutiérrez which is
reached by a No 50 bus from near the Club Andino's headquarters
in Bariloche. The bus terminates beside a small kiosk at the lake
end. This is a popular spot for swimming, fishing and windsurfing
during summer weekends. There are two good camp sites nearby,
both with excellent facilities: Camping 'W' beside the Bariloche to
El Bolsón road about 200 metres beyond the turning to the lake
head; Autocamping, beside the lake about two kilometres beyond the
place where the bus stops.

Directions
Lago Gutiérrez to Refugio Frey   Starting from the place where the
No 50 bus terminates, take the lefthand of two dirt tracks ahead.
This is signposted Autocamping. Follow this for about two
kilometres and just before the camp site you will reach the house of
the *guardaparque*. He will give you information on the area and the
state of the trail.

Take the trail which forks off right just before the camp site and
is signposted to Refugio Frey. Follow the white waymarkers which
take you through the woods around the camp site and onto a narrow
track which climbs steadily. After about 30 minutes you come to the
top of a rise. Ignore the path leading right and carry on down the
path which crosses a stream. This is a good place to top up water
bottles before the hot climb ahead.

The trail continues as a dusty track through open bush country.
After 15 minutes you reach a T-junction indicated on a stone. Take
the left turning, following the red paint markings and ignoring a
path to the left 20 minutes on. Soon the trail enters the woods again
and climbs steeply. The trail is joined from the right by the trail to

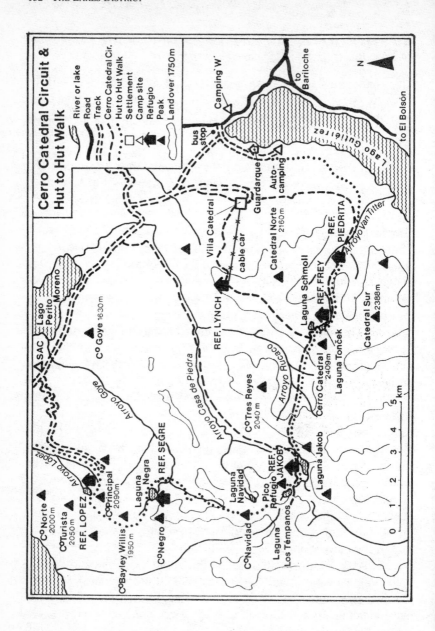

Cerro Catedral Circuit & Hut to Hut Walk

River or lake
Road
Track
Cerro Catedral Cir.
Hut to Hut Walk
Settlement
Camp site
Refugio
Peak
Land over 1750m

N

to Bariloche

to El Bolsón

Lago Gutiérrez

Camping 'W'

bus stop

Guardaque

Auto-camping

Villa Catedral

cable car

Catedral Norte 2160m

REF. PIEDRITA

Arroyo Van Titter

REF. FREY

Laguna Schmoll

REF. LYNCH

Catedral Sur 2388m

Cerro Catedral 2409m

Laguna Tonček

Arroyo Rucaco

Co Tres Reyes 2040 m

Arroyo Casa de Piedra

Lago Perito Moreno

Co Goye 1630m

SAC

Arroyo Goye

Laguna Jakob

REF. SEGRE

Laguna Negra

Co Principal 2090m

Bayley Willis 1950 m

Co Negro

REF. LOPEZ

Co Turista 2050m

Co Norte 2000m

Arroyo López

Laguna Navidad

Co Navidad

Pico REF. JAKOB Refugio

Laguna Los Témpanos

0 1 2 3 4 5 km

Villa Catedral and a little further on you cross the Arroyo van Titter over a tree trunk bridge. Here at last you can cool your feet in its clear waters. Fifteen minutes on you pass the picturesque Refugio Piedrita (see page 130).

Another one and a half hour's walk up the steep and dusty trail brings you to Refugio Frey at the eastern end of Laguna Tonček. This two storey stone building holds 40 people. Good camping spots can be found to the left (south) of the lake from where you can admire the impressive pinnacles of Cerro Catedral (2409 metres) as you cool off with a refreshing dip in the lake.

Refugio Frey to Refugio Jakob Walk up either side of the Laguna Tonček to the northern end where a stream tumbles down a rocky slope and enters the lake. Follow the splashes of red paint up this slope, keeping the stream to your left and heading for what looks like a saddle. This is in fact the rim of a basin containing Laguna Schmoll. Follow the path left of Laguna Schmoll which climbs out of the basin to the northwest. The route is well marked with splashes of red paint. Before you reach the top of the ridge, the path levels off and veers right through a small canyon, emerging after a few hundred metres on a rocky ledge high above Arroyo Rucaco. Follow the arrow and sign for Refugio Jakob, painted on a rock. The path doubles back on itself before dropping westwards down steep scree into the Rucaco valley. Slide down as best you can and when you meet the first vegetation follow a dry river gully. The descent takes about 30 minutes. Head west along the path on the left of the valley, crossing an area of wet, boggy meadow before entering the trees. Red paint markings lead you through the woods across several small streams and good camping spots. As you emerge from the trees, the path climbs steadily, crossing a stony plateau after about 30 minutes then scrambling up steep scree to the top of the ridge above. Here, at 1850 metres, you have magnificent views: to the southeast, the towers of Cerro Catedral; ahead below you, Laguna Jakob; and to the northwest, the steep wooded slopes bordering Arroyo Casa de Piedra. To reach Refugio Jakob you will have to scramble down loose scree for about an hour. We found good camp sites near the southwest end of Laguna Jakob beside a crystalline stream which flows into the lake from a valley to the north.

Refugio Jakob to Refugio Segre Before attempting this section, the wildest and remotest of the circuit, you should consult the warden at Refugio Jakob who will tell you the state of the route and show you photographs to help you identify the correct path.

From Laguna Jakob follow the red paint arrows and circles indicating the trail to Laguna Los Témpanos. This passes to the north side of Laguna Jakob. Follow the path over rocks and boulders for about 20 minutes until you come to the top of a rocky ridge. Here a cairn on the left indicates the path down to Laguna Los Témpanos. The path now turns right over the rocky ridge between Laguna Los Témpanos and Laguna Jakob and leads north towards the pointed summit of Pico Refugio. In 1988 the route was not waymarked after leaving the path to Laguna Los Témpanos, although the odd cairn reassured us we were not the first to have been this way. After about 20 minutes you reach the first of a series of three steep rock faces which can be seen in the profile of Pico Refugio from Refugio Jakob. Walk left under the first rock face for about 100 metres until you reach the foot of an obvious gully down which a stream trickles. Follow the gully up. You may find it easier to scramble up the rock to the right rather than climbing up the gully itself. This is not difficult but you should tread carefully. Below lies Laguna Los Témpanos and ahead you can see two peaks. Follow the gully to the point where it opens out and is filled with loose boulders at the base of the twin pinnacles. Cross the ridge in a small col beneath a third rocky pinnacle northwest of the other two and go down the gully on the other side for a short while before beginning a traverse beneath the east face of this third peak. Head across the rock basin ahead towards a small scree-filled col in the ridge to the north, identified from the following profile:

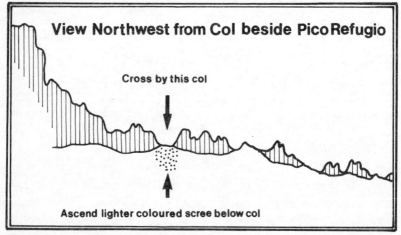

View Northwest from Col beside Pico Refugio

Cross by this col

Ascend lighter coloured scree below col

Several rocky gullies cut into the rock basin, but they remain hidden until you get close to them. By keeping fairly high you can easily climb in and out of these gullies and arrive beneath the col without having lost too much height. Scramble up to the col where you enjoy views of Cerro Catedral behind you, Cerro Negro to the north, Cerro Navidad to the northwest, and just to the left of that, in the far distance, the pointed peak of Cerro Puntiagudo in Chile. It should take about two and a half hours to reach this point from the *refugio*.

The next hour is spent negotiating the screes above Laguna Navidad and requires special care. Losing only a little height, head left (west) around the head of the valley, staying below the pinnacled ridge top. Pass below the rock buttress about two thirds of the way round before turning left and clambering back up the scree to gain the ridge which leads to the summit of Cerro Navidad. Avoid any pinnacles along the way by keeping left of the ridge.

From the top of Cerro Navidad, continue north across the boulder fields to the righthand side of Cerro Negro ahead. This will bring you to the top of Arroyo Navidad which you must descend. The path is steep and tough, but if you have got this far on the walk you will be well used to such conditions. We found gaiters useful for keeping stones out of our boots on these descents. At first you will have to slide carefully down scree but this later turns into boulders. As you follow the stream down you will need to pick the easiest route by constantly crossing from one side to the other. After an hour to an hour and a half you reach the top of the tree line. From here a series of cairns lead you away from the stream to your left and across a grassy meadow. The path eventually leads back to the river where there are good camping spots. From here the path is again marked with red paint splashes and leads you down to a T-junction with the main path up Arroyo Casa de Piedra. Turning left you embark on the laborious slog up a zigzag path to Refugio Segre (also known as Refugio Italia). This has been visible since the beginning of the climb down the Arroyo Navidad. If your muscles allow, you can save time by scrambling straight up the stream gully left of the path for the first section. It takes an hour to reach the lip of the corrie containing Laguna Negra and the Refugio Segre. You can camp at the southeast end of the lake.

Refugio Segre to Refugio López   Follow the well marked path which crosses the rocky north side of Laguna Negra. In places you will have to scramble and a fixed rope may be helpful. The path heads north from the end of the lake and follows the stream which feeds the lake before climbing to the broad ridge to the left of Bayley Willis (1950 metres). Avoiding the summit, follow the path which leads northwest from the mountain's west face to a second col. Pick your way down through the scree and boulders, watching carefully for red paint markings. Keep left of the green boggy area before the valley bottom. There are plenty of camping spots in the valley.

The path now climbs steeply in and out of scrub and trees signposted with red paint markings. The trail then levels off slightly as you cross a stony area at the foot of the stone shoot which leads out of the valley to the right of its head wall. It takes an hour to an hour and a half of careful scrambling up the boulder-filled gully to reach a ridge.

Once you are on the ridge, Refugio López is now only an hour away so it is worth making a small diversion to the left (north) to climb Cerro Turista (2050 metres) where you will find a seat from where to admire the fine views of Bariloche and Lago Nahuel Huapí below.

Retracing your steps along the ridge top, you will see the path down marked with red and silver arrows. This descends the northeastern side of the ridge. You will pass a rock knoll and a small lake which provides the *refugio* below with water. After further scrambling down a rocky gully you reach the spectacularly positioned Refugio López. In summer weekends it is frequented by day trippers and has a simple cafeteria service. If you wish to camp, the best place is about 15 minutes below the *refugio* in the woods where there are level clearings. It takes nearly two hours to reach the road to Colonia Suiza so depending how you feel, you may decide to descend the same day or linger a little longer in the mountains.

To get to Bariloche, take the well worn track from Refugio López to the main road to Colonia Suiza. The No 10 bus passes here several times a day for Bariloche. If you turn right and walk a further one and a half kilometres you will reach the well organized SAC camp site where you can ask about bus times and buy refreshments in their small store.

Practical information
Time/rating The huts are ideally situated one day's walk from each other. The circuit can be done in four days, or five if the last night is spent in Refugio López. None of the scrambling is difficult but requires care and can be hair-raising at times. The route is not recommended in reverse because of the tedious ascent to Refugio López but it would be possible.

Preparations Be sure to consult the Club Andino in Bariloche about snow conditions before setting out. You can buy biscuits, beer and bottled drinks at the *refugios* but you should buy your main meals in Bariloche. A compass, plus warm and waterproof clothing are essential. Gaiters are useful.

Maps Ask at the Club Andino for a copy of their 1:100,000 (approx) map. Although it is rather crude and not 100 per cent accurate, it does show the positions of ridges and peaks and certainly enabled us to find the way.

LAKE TO LAKE WALK, BARILOCHE AREA
by John and Christine Myerscough

This walk takes you through a stunningly beautiful area of Argentina which has the advantage of being totally wild. Here, in complete peace, you will enjoy breathtaking mountain peaks, sparkling blue lakes and cascading streams. The section between Laguna Azul, nestling between smooth polished rock walls, and Laguna Cab was perhaps the most exhilarating walks we did in Argentina. Given good weather, which is common early in the year, you will be able to see beyond Mount

Tronador into Chile where the perfect cone of Volcán Osorno rises above Lago Todos los Santos.

Like the Hut to Hut walk this tough, challenging hike should only be attempted by experienced walkers. You will need a tent. The best camping spots are beside the lakes or beside mountain streams. You will find firewood at all the camping sites we mention but it is far better to carry your own stove and leave these unspoilt beauty spots as they are. You should visit the Club Andino in Bariloche before setting out to check on snow conditions and to get a photocopy of their rather basic map of the area. Drinking water is available all along the walk. You could extend the Lake Todos los Santos to Lake Mascardi walk by joining this walk near Hotel Tronador (see page 140).

Directions
Lago Mascardi (east) to Lago Mascardi (west) via Laguna Llum
The walks starts from the northern tip of the east arm of Lago Mascardi. From Bariloche take the Charta Co bus which leaves

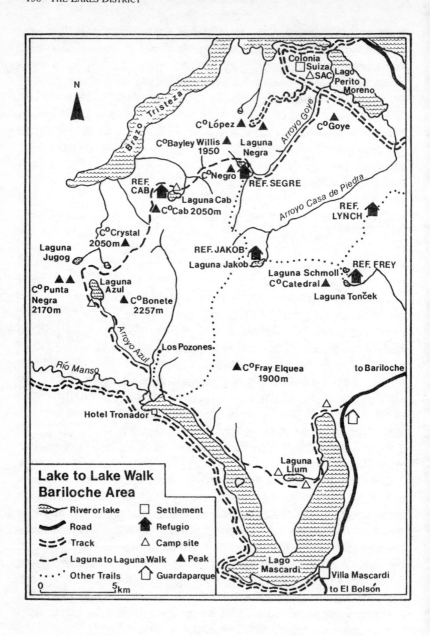

N

Brazo Tristeza

Colonia
Suiza
△SAC
Lago
Perito
Moreno

Arroyo Goye

C°López ▲
C°Goye

C°Bayley Willis ▲
1950
Laguna
Negra

REF. SEGRE

C°Negro

Arroyo Casa de Piedra

REF.
CAB

REF.
LYNCH

Laguna Cab
C°Cab 2050m

C°Crystal
2050m▲

REF. JAKOB

Laguna
Jugog

Laguna Jakob

Laguna Schmoll
C°Catedral ▲

REF. FREY

Laguna Tonček

▲ ▲

C°Punta
Negra
2170m
△

Laguna
Azul

C°Bonete
2257m

Arroyo Azul

Los Pozones

Río Manso

▲C°Fray Elquea
1900m

to Bariloche

△

Hotel Tronador ⌂

Laguna
Llum

△

**Lake to Lake Walk
Bariloche Area**

≈≈≈ River or lake   ☐ Settlement
━━━ Road   ⌂ Refugio
╍╍╍ Track   △ Camp site
╌╌╌ Laguna to Laguna Walk ⌂ Guardaparque
∙∙∙∙∙ Other Trails   ▲ Peak

0 ————— 5 km

Lago
Mascardi

Villa Mascardi
to El Bolsón

from near the tourist office on Calle Mitre. Ask the driver to stop at the *guardería* at the north end of the lake. Here you can ask for further information if the office is open.

The route starts on a track, about 100 metres back down the road from the *guardería*, which leads to the lake shore. Here a wooded area offers excellent camping. Walk along the lake shore for half an hour and then up the trail which climbs a steep bank through trees before levelling off again. The path is not waymarked but is well defined and wide enough for two people to walk side by side. It passes through a gate and winds through picturesque woods, affording occasional views of the lake below. After another half-hour you drop down to the lake edge and cross a small stream over a tree trunk bridge. Turn right and follow the trail left of the stream. You soon start climbing away from the lake and enter thick vegetation. About 45 minutes after leaving Lago Mascardi you emerge at the eastern end of the secluded and peaceful Laguna Llum. From here the trail follows the left (southern) side of the lake eventually bringing you out at the western end. It is possible to camp in small clearings in the woods that lead down to the lake. The walk through the trees to the western end takes about 30 to 40 minutes. Here there is a ramshackle wooden corral enclosing an apple orchard. There is also a dilapidated shelter and plenty of nice camping areas. The path meanders over fairly level ground but at times you may have to push through vegetation where it has become overgrown. Fifteen minutes from the orchard the trail climbs through bamboo forest, eventually bringing you out onto a rocky crest with fine views of Mount Tronador. If you walk to the high point to the left you also get a splendid view of Lago Mascardi. The path goes straight over the crest, waymarked with a cairn. Follow the soil track down through thick bamboo, being careful not to lose your way as there are no waymarks. Forty-five minutes below the top you reach a small stream. From here a faint path takes you over a small ridge from where you glimpse Lago Mascardi below. Thirty minutes from the stream you should be above the lake once more. The trail is indistinct in places and takes you over many fallen trees but occasional paint markings reassure you that you are on the right path. After walking for an hour above the lake the path drops down again to the shore where you cross a small stream. Continue another one and a half hours above the lake until you reach a river. Here the trail meets a path from the right which leads up to Refugio Jakob. Turn left and follow the river to the lake where there is a bridge of fallen tree trunks and a sign to Laguna Jakob. Here there are plenty of spaces to camp and you can enjoy views of Cerro Bonete (2257 metres) and Cresta de Galle with the snowy top of Mount Tronador peeping out in the distance. Across the lake can be seen the luxury Hotel Tronador and its attractive gardens. If you are lucky a fisherman may row you across for a cool beer.

Lago Mascardi (west) to Laguna Azul   Continue round the lake and after 30 minutes you will come to a sign saying *Los Pozones* (Deep Pools). Turn right along the path (marked with bamboo sticks) which heads towards Cerro Bonete. Soon you reach a broad river where there is an arrow pointing right. Follow this path which soon drops down to a river which you can cross without getting wet feet. The trail then climbs steeply upstream. Soon it levels off and veers left away from the river. Thirty minutes after the first river crossing the path again climbs gently through the trees along the left bank of another river, the Arroyo Azul. This flows from Laguna Azul through a steep sided twisting gorge. The trail is not waymarked, but when we went up it it had recently been cleared so that horses could pass. The path leads to the foot of Cerro Bonete although the view of this giant mountain is obscured by vegetation. After following the Arroyo Azul for an hour a sign saying *cruce* indicates where you should cross. A soft leafy path climbs along the right bank of the river and after 15 minutes opens into a flat grassy area with a waterfall trickling down a rocky face on the left.

The trail continues on the righthand side of the river which now crashes down in a series of cascades while to your right are the forbidding grey crags of Cerro Bonete. After about 30 minutes you reach the point where the Arroyo Azul rushes over great slabs of rock. The path is right of the slabs, marked by little piles of stones. Soon, however, it crosses to the left side of the river where it climbs through trees before emerging onto more steep rocky slabs. After scrambling up these you reach a small level wooded area. The path is marked with cairns and passes through dwarf trees before reaching Laguna Azul, a deep blue lake situated in a magnificent rock amphitheatre. Good camping can be found in a grassy clearing left of the lake, close to its exit stream.

Laguna Azul to Laguna Cab   The trail continues along the left (southwest) side of Laguna Azul and has been cleared through small patches of dwarf trees. It is not waymarked but is easy to follow if you look for the cuts. Cross a stream that comes down off the slabs under Cerro Punta Negra and 30 minutes later you reach the northwest end of the lake where you start to climb the slabs in a northwest direction. The slabs provide good grip and after a strenuous climb of one hour bring you out onto the curved ridge high above Laguna Azul. There may be patches of snow up here but these can easily be avoided. If you have time, excursions up Cerro Punta Negra and Cerro Bonete could be made from this point but you would need a day to climb either. From the top of this ridge you can see the small Lago Jugog to your left. On the other side of the ridge you can see Brazo la Tristeza below you, while to the right the rugged outline of Cerro Cristal is visible. Go right and cross the ridge to the east above Laguna Azul. From the shallow col below Cerro Bonete make your way down in a northeasterly direction towards a little unnamed lake and climb the screes on the south side of Cerro Cristal. It should take about one hour to reach the ridge from where you have a splendid view of Tronador to the west. Head north along its rocky ridge towards the pointed summit of Cerro Cristal but before you start the final climb cross the slabs to the right and head towards the northeast ridge coming off Cerro Cristal. It should take about 30 minutes to cross the slabs.

Follow the northeast ridge of Cerro Cristal down to the grassy basin below which there are plenty of camping spots. This takes about an hour. Head northeast up the scree slopes to the ridge which is just under 2000 metres and looks down on Laguna Cab. The climb, which is rocky and steep near the top, takes about an hour. Go left along the ridge that circles Laguna Cab. Below you to the right the *refugio* can be seen nestling next to the feeder stream into Laguna Cab. Follow the ridge all the way round to the right and down its end slopes to the lake shore beside the exit stream. The descent, which may mean some bushwhacking through dwarf trees, should take one and a half hours. Here you will find plenty of level ground and fireplaces for camping.

Laguna Cab to Laguna Negra From the exit stream at the north end of Laguna Cab follow the well used path down the left side of the stream for 15 minutes until you see a yellow marker which indicates the crossing to the right above a waterfall. The path then climbs out of some woods into an area of open mountain. Cross a sandy path eastwards which is waymarked with strips of coloured plastic. The area appears to have been damaged by fire as a lot of burnt trees litter the slopes. This clearing allows you to view your next and final climb which will bring you out above Laguna Negra. The path turns northeast and goes steeply down a sandy track for 15 minutes towards a tree covered area. The trail, marked with splashes of paint on trees and stones, now winds its way down to the valley bottom where you cross a stream by a tree trunk bridge. When you come to a T-junction, take the trail which goes north to the right and climbs gently until you hear a stream to the right. Fifteen minutes from the valley bottom you drop down and cross the river following the plastic ribbon marking on a tree. The trail now climbs steeply eastwards away from the stream and up through trees to the massif of Bayley Willis. After about one hour you reach a corrie filled with small trees. Follow the lefthand side of the corrie and climb the scree slopes of the northeast side which lead to the ridge above Laguna Negra. This takes about 30 minutes. Cairns indicate the way on the ridge. To make your way down, head northeast and after 15 minutes you should reach the eastern edge of Laguna Negra. Follow the well marked path left of the lake which passes over slabs and boulders close to the shore and leads to the palatial Refugio Segre.

From here it is 16 kilometres downhill to civilization. The steep zigzag track soon turns into a pleasant trail beside the Arroyo Negro which swells to become Arroyo Goye. Eventually you reach Colonia Suiza. Here there is a choice of three excellent camp sites or a bus back to the pizzas and chocolate of Bariloche. From Laguna Negra to Colonia Suiza takes about three hours.

Practical information
Time/rating You should allow four to five complete days for the walk, much of which is tough. In winter the higher sections of the hike would be snow covered, making it a serious undertaking.

Preparations A tent and compass are essential, as are warm and waterproof clothing. A small machete might be useful for clearing overgrown vegetation.

Maps No decent maps are available although a blurred photocopy of a 1:100,000 map can be bought from the Club Andino in Bariloche.

Chapter Ten

The Carretera Austral

Until a few years ago the 'cold jungle' south of Puerto Montt remained unknown and uninhabitable to all but a handful of isolated fishing villages. Sea travellers caught tantalising glimpses of dense forests through the mist and rain as their ship slid through the channels between the many islands, but in 1988 a road was opened as far south as Cochrane. This is Chile's Carretera Austral.

Rivers slice through this rugged landscape and two must be crossed by ferry which normally only operate between December and March (check in Puerto Montt before heading south). This wettest of regions (they say in Puerto Aisén it rains 370 days a year) has pockets of sunshine: Chile Chico, on Lago Carrera and near the Jeinimeni National Park (described later), manages 300 sunny days a year.

CYCLING THE CARRETERA AUSTRAL
by Nick Cotton

Between November and March there can be few finer long distance mountain bike tours in the world than the Carretera Austral which runs 1000 kilometres south from Puerto Montt to Cochrane. It is an unpaved road which heads south past glaciers and snowcapped mountains, lakes of every colour, rivers and waterfalls through dense exuberant vegetation with glimpses of humming birds. It is a cross between Switzerland, the Wild West, the Scottish coast and a tropical jungle. If that is not enough to tempt you, the wine is cheap, the people friendly and getting there is pretty straightforward.

To claim that our trip was all a bed of roses would be misleading, but the intermittent wind or rain or rough roads were variations on a theme rather than a negation of the theme itself. We never questioned why we were there: a quick look around would tell us: minor roads in Europe are made for cycle touring, this road was made for mountain bikes!

Getting the bikes to South America was easier than expected, and a connecting flight took us from Santiago to Punta Arenas. The first part of our trip round Tierra del Fuego and into Patagonia was a mistake, or at least not something I would recommend to someone who had a limited time in South America on a mountain bike. In this enormous continent distances are so vast that you have to be selective and as far as we could see, cycling the Carretera Austral was a joy in itself whereas in Patagonia we had crossed a lot of dross to get from one national park to the next.

The idea behind the recent construction of the Carretera Austral (begun in 1980, still being built), was to link together isolated settlements colonised in the last hundred years to the more populated part of Chile north of Puerto Montt. This is why there is still a Wild West feel to the place. Men ride around on horses wearing wide-brimmed hats. Pairs of oxen pull along carts with wooden wheels. The stores in the small villages are as you would imagine frontier town commerce in the late 19th century. Houses are made of wood and the land is still being tamed and cleared. There are pumas in the hills which attack flocks of sheep (but not humans, honest!) We had to take rafts across the bigger rivers where bridges had not yet been built.

It was at one of these river crossings that we saw a vehicle with an exotic motif painted on the side and the words "Anihue — The Cold Jungle." This was the phrase I had been looking for to describe the cross between Scotland (the climate) and the Amazon (the vegetation). Bamboo and hardwood combine to form an impenetrable mass of luxuriant green vegetation. This talk of jungle may suggest spiders and snakes, but in that respect, Chile is safer than Britain with no poisonous snakes and no animals dangerous to man.

Our Carretera Austral trip started at Chile Chico on the southern shore of Lake General Carrera, the second largest lake in South America. For four days we followed the shoreline west then north along cliff roads still being blasted out, over suspension bridges and through small villages. To our right the lake shimmered blue or was whipped into white horses by the fierce westerly winds which blow down there. We passed by road-building crews who waved us through where cars could not yet pass, pushed our laden bikes up horrendously steep rough hills yet to be smoothed out, flew down the other side, breaking the pannier racks once again (thanks be to thee, O roll of white zinc oxide tape, for saving us once again) and camped at night in meadows by rivers. Being as far south as England is north, there is plenty of daylight in the summertime (November to March) and it does not freeze at night so camping was a pretty pleasant experience.

On the fifth day we climbed to a small pass at 600 metres and headed east. The descent into Villa Castillo we had been looking forward to turned out to be dreadful: the awful road surface meant that we could never let rip and our wrists and arms were more tired at the end of the day than our legs. A good quantity of beers and cherries and cream set us up for the climb the next day to the highest point of the route at 3500 feet. For the next day and a half, we encountered more traffic as we headed north to Coihaique, the only big town on the whole route, where we ate ourselves silly, restocked supplies, changed money, got some clothes washed, and fixed up our bikes.

From Coihaique, rested, we glided downhill on the only paved section of the whole route to Puerto Aisén amidst truly wondrous vegetation and waterfalls. We encountered our first rain of the trip which was with us for the next six days. We soon learned that everything must be double wrapped in plastic bags and that good thermal underwear is as important as good waterproofs to keep you warm in the rain.

Our final side trip was to the hot, thermal baths at Termas del Amarillo, near to Chaitén. A short climb took us to a paradise of pink flowers and big baths of hot water shooting out of pipes to pummel those aching muscles. We had hoped to continue north to Puerto Montt by road, but the river ferries were not operating in March so we took a boat direct from Chaitén to Puerto Montt.

JEINIMENI NATIONAL PARK
by J M Bibby

Only 60 kilometres south of Chile Chico lies the Jeinimeni National Park. Here you will find breathtaking snow-capped peaks, impressive cliffs, waterfalls and small glaciers set around the calypso blue and emerald green Lagos Jeinimeni and Verde.

Activities include fishing for salmon and rainbow trout, trekking (or rather trailblazing as there are few paths), rowing, and just enjoying the tranquillity. Treks range from three or four day valley walks to steep and tough scrambles up one of the few accessible 1800m peaks. The IGM map *Lago Verde* is essential — buy it in Santiago.

Access is generally only feasible between November and March due to river levels. You can seek a lift with one of the two wood-carrying lorries which visit the park frequently — try Juan Viega in the shop next to the CONAF office in Chile Chico.

There is a small entrance fee payable at the parkwardens' hut. A couple of picnic shelters, a rowing boat and plenty of firewood are available for use by campers.

Getting to Chile Chico from Puerto Ibáñez

The owner of the ferry from Puerto Ibáñez to Chile Chico is Mar del Sur, who may change the timetable after consultation. Cost is about $3 per person plus about $30 per vehicle.

Minibuses run from outside El Gran Calafate in Prat Street, Coyhaique, to connect with the ferry at Ibáñez. You need to book personally with the minibus driver on the afternoon before you wish to travel. Cost is approximately $7 for the three hour journey.

Suggested hikes

All timings and routes are taken from and back to Lago Verde base camp. In each case further exploration may give alternative means of access to the various peaks and glaciers.

Huemules Rock

Time: Three hours

Description: A steep scramble up rock and scrub to the 1257m peak above the camp site with views over lakes and down the Valle Hermoso to the glaciers.

Route: Either along the ridge from the corner of Lago Verde or up a gentler grassy slope from Estero La Gloria where the bank rises to form a grassy ledge (see below).

Camino Camano and Col del Caballo Blanco

Time: Two and a half hours

Description: A pleasant walk along a wooded path with two river crossings to the col which gives views over Lago Verde and the Valle Hermoso glacier.

Route: From the NW end of the grassy plain lying to the NE of the camp site, follow the path through the trees, turning right onto the river plain at a small boulder. Cross the river before it hits the cliff, and cross back onto the left bank where the bank rises to form a grassy ledge strewn with dead trees. Follow the path into the wood where it turns sharply uphill, reaching the col after passing under a large white cliff.

Glacier trek
Time: Two to five days (50km in total)
Description: Treks up valleys to the lakes at the bottom of glaciers: Valle Hermoso, Lagunas Escondida and Ventisquero.

There are numerous river crossings, mostly knee-deep. The lakes themselves are barren and surrounded by scree and moraine. Technical equipment is needed to climb onto the glaciers.
Route: From Col del Caballo Blanco (see above) follow the horse track down to the western end of Lago Verde. Cross both rivers (to avoid battling through trees, scrub and bog) and proceed up the valleys along the river plain and through woodland.

Good camp sites can be found behind CONAF hut and in mature woodland, for example on the western edge of Valle Hermoso, the eastern side of Estero Los Ventisqueros and at the bottom of the valley which descends from Laguna Escondida.

Wisdom Peak
Time: Six-seven hours
Description: Steep scramble through trees and up fairly stable scree to the 1839m peak with views over Argentina, lakes and mountains.
Route: Follow the dry river valley up from Estero La Gloria and continue up the ridge to the summit.

An alternative ascent can be made from the northern end of Lago Jeinimeni, although this involves negotiating a gulley of loose rock near the summit — a safety rope is required.

La Cascada (waterfall walk)
Time: Two hours
Description: A scramble at a gentle gradient over boulders and through trees to superb waterfalls falling into clear pools.
Route: Cross the Río Verde at a shallow point just below the entrance of the stream from the waterfall. The crossing is knee-deep, but fast-flowing even in dry weather. Proceed up the stream through the wood on the western side of the valley.

Cerro Peñón

Time: Seven hours

Description: A steep scramble up and across forested and scree slopes, negotiating waterfalls until the valley opens onto a grassy plain before a steep scree ascent to Cerro Peñón (1986m). We did not proceed to Peñón but climbed onto the ridge for views over Lago Verde and Valle Hermoso.

Route: Set of as for the waterfall (above) but cut up the right hand side of the valley to circumvent the waterfall. Proceed upstream to the summit.

Raleigh Peak

Time: Six hours to do the peak from the camp site.

Description: A beautiful valley walk up Estero San Antonio, crossing the knee-deep river numerous times, followed by very steep but fairly easy ascent to the 1784m summit which gives good views of Cerro Peñón and ridges. Route onwards to Peñón looked blocked by cliffs.

Route: Follow the path which crosses Estero San Antonio many times to a camp site in trees, from which there is a direct ascent to the summit.

Chapter Eleven

Patagonia

by Hilary Bradt and Clare Hargreaves

The country remained the same, and was extremely uninteresting. The complete similarity of the productions throughout Patagonia is one of its most striking characteristics. The level plains of arid shingle support the same stunted and dwarf plants; and in the valleys the same thorn-bearing bushes grow. Everywhere we see the same birds and insects. Even the very banks of the river and of the clear streamlets which entered it, were scarcely enlivened by a brighter tint of green. The curse of sterility is on the land.
Charles Darwin, *The Voyage of the Beagle*, April 22, 1834.

Patagonia probably takes its name from *patagones*, meaning big feet. This is possibly a reference to a race of Indians who lived here and had a habit of wearing huge boots and stuffing them with grass for insulation which made their feet look disproportionately large. Another explanation is that Magellan named the land after *Gran Patagón*, a monster in a contemporary Spanish tale. Either way, the name stuck, and the area has in its time attracted a host of explorers, outlaws and eccentrics, and more recently, tourists.

Patagonia was originally the name given to the area of Argentina south of the Río Colorado, east of the Andes, and north of the Straits of Magellan. Today, however, the term is generally used to describe the whole of the Southern Cone of South America including both Chile and Argentina.

Scenically, Patagonia is a land of contrasts. The sterile, featureless plains on the Argentine side, which provoked Darwin's scathing remarks quoted above, provide some of the most boring views in the world. The *cordillera* of the Andes and the labyrinth of fjords and glaciers on the Chilean side offer some of the finest. The massifs of Fitz Roy and Paine, in the far south, must surely be the most beautiful in the Americas. The area is also rich in wildlife, described in fascinating detail by Darwin in *The Voyage of the*

17: Patagonia (136)

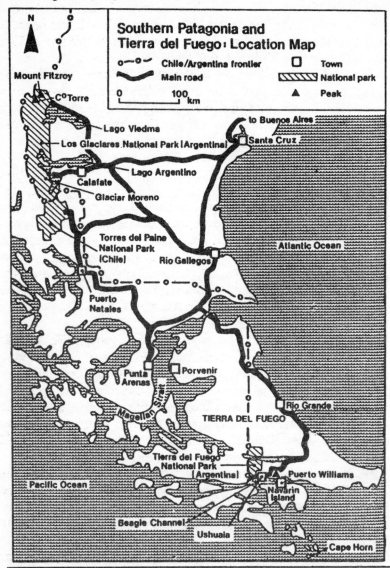

Southern Patagonia and Tierra del Fuego: Location Map

- o—o— Chile/Argentina frontier
- ⌇⌇⌇ Main road
- □ Town
- ▨▨ National park
- ▲ Peak

0 ___ 100 km

WHERE TO STAY IN PUNTA ARENAS AND PUERTO NATALES

Hotel Jose Noguiera, Bories 959, Punta Arenas (tel 248840/fax 248832). Central, 100-year-old hotel. En suite bathrooms throughout, plus several suites, with lounge and jacuzzi. 1996-97 room rates (inc breakfast): US$151 single, $180 double, $232 triple, $277 suite (all +18% tax).

Hotel Costaustralis, Puerto Natales (50-rooms) Seafront hotel with restaurant, bar, and cafeteria. Trekking, fishing trips and excursions to Milodon caves, Balmaceda and Serrano glaciers and Torres del Paine National Park arranged.

Beagle. Guanacos, rheas and the Patagonian fox and hare are frequently seen in the south, while Península Valdés, on the east coast, is one of the best places for viewing seals and marine birds in the whole of South America, and has recently become famous through television films of killer whales at work here.

The main settlement on the Chilean side is Punta Arenas on the Magellan Strait. Because of the area's rugged terrain, this can only be reached by air, by ship from Puerto Montt, or overland from Argentina. The main towns on the Argentinian side are Río Gallegos, Santa Cruz and Comodoro Rivadavia, in southern Patagonia, and Trelew in northern Patagonia.

Punta Arenas, located at the tip of the Chilean mainland looking across the Strait of Magellan to Tierra del Fuego, is a sleepy city of around 140,000 people. Once a penal colony, the city's flimsy multi-coloured corrugated iron houses and their gardens of lupins and marigolds have an air of incongruous impermanence. You will see ample evidence of the hardy European settlers who moved here at the end of the last century, particularly Yugoslavs, whose descendants still form a significant proportion of the city's population. Punta Arenas is an important naval base. The discovery of oil in the region has provided new found wealth.

The only other settlement you are likely to visit in Chilean Patagonia is Puerto Natales, 254 kilometres north of Punta Arenas. Buffetted by the winds which whistle down Last Hope Sound, this bleak ramshackle town seems even more incongruous and impermanent than Punta Arenas. Earlier this century the British built a meat-packing and tanning factory here and in the Plaza de Armas you can see the miniature steam engine built in Bristol in 1920 which was used to transport the meat and hides to the pier.

Puerto Natales is a useful jumping-off point for the Torres del Paine National Park 150km to the north, to which there is a good regular bus service. The *M/N Puerto Eden* links the town with Puerto Montt, a four-day trip. The vessel's operator, Navimag, has its Puerto Natales office at Avenida Pedro Mont 380 (tel 411 421/fax 411 642).

The cities in Argentine Patagonia offer little interest, unless you happen to take a fascination in oil extraction and refining techniques. The most important is Comodoro Rivadavia, a boom city whose 120,000 inhabitants live almost exclusively off the oil and petrochemicals industries. On December 13 it celebrates Petroleum Day. If you have the misfortune to get stuck here, make sure you have a few novels left unread and head for the beach, Rada Tilly, five kilometres south of the city.

WALES IN PATAGONIA

by Hilary Bradt

Trying to find the Welsh flavour of Chubut had been disappointing. We had been ticked off in the Welsh Tea Shop for propping our backpacks against the wall, and there was nothing in Trelew to make us feel we were in Pembrokeshire, or even Cardiff. Gaiman seemed more promising, but hitchhiking was slow and we arrived in the late evening, irritable, and with nowhere to stay. We walked down the street arguing about whether to sleep in a partly constructed building we had just passed, or to find a field on the outskirts of town to set up our tent (hotels were too expensive). Our raised voices attracted attention and to my embarrassment a man materialized before us and said: 'You need somewhere to stay, then? Come back to my house — I'm fed up with the bloody Spanish.' The accent was strongly Welsh, and we accepted.

Politely masking her surprise, his pretty Argentine wife greeted us then launched into an animated discussion with her husband. I was depressed at my poor Spanish: I could not follow any of the conversation. Gwyn turned to us. 'Sorry you couldn't understand that. We have to speak in Welsh: it's our common language. María doesn't speak English and I don't speak Spanish. We want you to come out to her parents' farm this weekend.'

María's family was one of the oldest in the Patagonian Welsh community. The women had always run the farm, and by tradition had been sent to Wales to finish their education and find a husband. Gwyn had not been in Argentina for long. We sat listening to stories of the old days (mercifully María's mother spoke English), how she would watch from the specially built turret for her father's return on horseback from the Big City, the lean years when beef prices were low and there was scarcely enough to eat, the time when the sun was blotted out for 24 hours by a volcanic eruption, and the determination of the tightly-knit community to keep the Welsh traditions alive. 'You know,' she said, 'I think we'll still be speaking Welsh in Patagonia when the language has died out in Wales.' She may be right.

At the bottom of the cherry orchard was a one-room adobe building. This had been María's grandfather's retreat, and it was left as it had been when he died the previous year at the age of 89: the hard couch covered with wool ponchos so he could sleep there if the noise of his family became too much, the kerosene lanterns which provided the only light, and his thousands of books lining the walls from top to bottom, several layers thick. He had been fluent in eight languages and conversant with another 10. When he went blind at the age of 80 he wasted no time in learning braille. Leaving the running of the farm to his wife, he immersed himself in his reading. It was he who had built the turret at the top of the house so he could watch out for his daughter as she rode back from town with the latest parcel of books that he had ordered from Europe and which had made their slow way to Buenos Aires by ship.

Our four day stay gave us an experience that could never be bought: the serendipity of travelling rough.

CHUBUT PROVINCE, NORTHERN PATAGONIA
by Clare Hargreaves and Hilary Bradt

On July 28 1865, 153 bedraggled Welsh immigrants landed on a desolate beach off what is now Puerto Madryn, in Chubut province, northern Argentine Patagonia. Led by a Lewis Jones, their dream was to found a New Wales in South America, where they would be allowed to speak their native tongue and escape the misery of the cramped mining valleys. But at first, life in Patagonia, 1400 kilometres south of Buenos Aires, was scarcely better than the one they had left behind: one bachelor who climbed the cliffs in search of food disappeared never to return, and the rock-hard barren landscape looked as if it would not nurture so much as a blade of grass. Within a few days the sheep brought down from the north were lost on the pampa and the semi-wild cattle of the Río Negro refused to be milked. Three weeks later the motley party pushed up the valley of the Río Chubut where they found flat cultivable land and the colony eventually prospered. The last Welsh contingent arrived in 1911.

If you visit Trelew (pronounced Treléo), 20 kilometres up the Río Chubut from Puerto Madryn, or Gaiman today you will still hear Welsh, although the language is slowly dying out as Welsh descendants intermarry with Argentines. However, many still sing in choirs at the Welsh non-conformist chapels, and they even hold their own annual Eisteddfod. Welsh tea houses, although not authentically Welsh, provide delicious cream teas which are quite a bizarre experience when you are in the depths of South America. Try the special *torta negra* (black cake), a delicious spicy fruit cake.

Trelew or Puerto Madryn are also the starting points to visit the Valdés peninsula, an anchor shaped projection of land jutting into the turbulent Atlantic Ocean which provides a home to the most plentiful wildlife in Patagonia. The plankton-rich Falkland Current washes the shores of the peninsula, providing food for the largest nursery of right whales in the world. Plankton are also eaten by fish which attract the peninsula's famous sealions, fur seals and elephant seals, and these in turn fall prey to the carnivorous killer whales that frequent the area. Fine wildlife can also be seen at Punta Tombo, 120 kilometres south of Trelew. However, a series of natural and man-made disasters have taken their toll on the wildlife populations. Firstly, the Hudson Volcano dumped two cubic miles of ash over the province, then a mysterious oil spill off the Valdés peninsula killed at least 16,000 penguins as they migrated to the area from Brazil. In recent years the number of fishing boats plying the area has increased enormously, threatening the delicate ecosystem. The Patagonia Nature Foundation has attempted to create an 18-mile marine reserve to protect the food supplies of the coastal animals that migrate to the area to breed.

If you go further up the Chubut valley you come to Esquel and Trevelin, pretty Welsh towns set in the lush foothills of the Andes where you can supplement cream teas with locally grown raspberries or peaches. From Esquel you can visit the Los Alerces National Park, famous for its larch trees, some of which are up to 2500 years old. Good walking can be done here. From Esquel you can also take the tourist train to the Nahuel Pan Indian reserve.

Getting there

All Argentina's airlines fly regularly to Trelew. There are also frequent buses. Regular buses also go to Gaiman, 18 kilometres west of Trelew.

Getting to the Valdés peninsula is tricky, and you may prefer to take a tour from Puerto Madryn. The best bet is to take a bus from 28 de Julio in Puerto Madryn to Puerto Pirámides. Or you can hitch, although we waited several hours for a lift before giving up. We were reminded of an old saying: 'If you want to see Patagonia, just sit still and it will all blow past you'. In fact it all blew onto us: into our eyes and up our noses. Eventually we hired a car at Trelew, but we have met many people who *have* hitched the journey successfully, and this is a place for sitting and watching, rather than driving. You will also have to hitch if you want to visit Punta Tombo, an hour and three quarters' drive from Trelew.

Esquel is reached by bus from Trelew, Bariloche, or Comodoro Rivadavia or you can fly with Aerolíneas or LADE. Unfortunately, whilst the Lagos del Sur train runs occasionally from Buenos Aires to Jacobacci (at least 31 hours) the narrow gauge steam train on to Esquel, as described by Paul Theroux in *The Old Patagonian Express*, no longer operates. There are regular buses from Esquel to Trevelin, 23 kilometres southwest.

Los Alerces National Park is reached by bus from Esquel, although you can visit part of it from Trevelin.

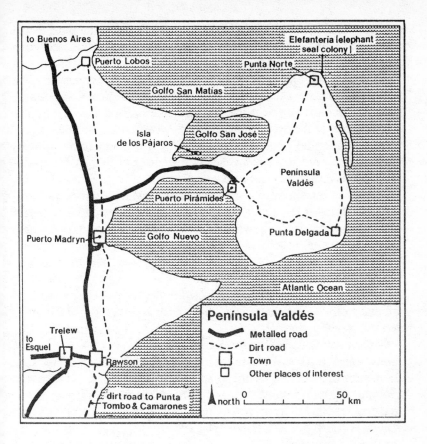

Península Valdés

Golfo San José, on the north side of the peninsula, is a deep bay providing two outstanding wildlife viewing areas: the Isla de los Pájaros ('Island of Birds') with numerous species of marine birds, including flamingos; and the marine sanctuary in the bay itself, which is a nursery for right whales and a hunting ground for killer whales and their relatives the dolphins.

Right whales arrive in Golfo San José in winter to mate, calve and raise their young. Once hunted to the brink of extinction (the name indicates that these were the 'right' whales to hunt because they moved slowly, floated when dead, and provided plenty of baleen or whalebone), these mammals enjoy complete protection here and are easily observed from the shore with the aid of telescopes which are provided free. With their barnacle-encrusted callosities they may not be the most attractive of animals, but are certainly among the most intelligent. Probably the best time to visit is in early November when you have a chance to watch the females with their newborn calves.

The handsome black and white killer whales (*orcas*) are smaller than right whales, but possess a fearsome set of 50 pointed teeth. They feed exclusively on warm-blooded creatures, and have become expert at taking young seals in the shallow water just off the beach.

Puerto Pirámides is the next place of interest, both for the eroded rocks which give it its name and the *lobería* or fur seal colony. There are camping facilities here.

On leaving the fur seals, most naturalists head for the *elefantería* at Punta Norte. Elephant seals are found all along the coast here, and of course the further you walk from the parking area, the better your chance of watching these marvellous animals in peace. Breeding time is first fortnight in August and the best time to see them is low tide.

If you continue on to Punta Delgada, at the south of the peninsula, you may well see killer whales. This is also a good area for viewing elephant seals and, if you are lucky, penguins. In Punta Delgada itself the viewing is not as good as Punta Norte.

Returning to Puerto Madryn along Route 2 you will pass a depression to the right of the road which is 35 metres below sea level and reputed to be the lowest point in South America.

Punta Tombo and Camarones
Not far from Península Valdés is a vast rookery of magellanic penguins. Nearly a million birds raise their chicks in burrows on Punta Tombo and Camarones during the summer months. Do not bother going after mid March as the penguins are 'off limits' as they prepare to return to the sea. Camarones has its own national park where guanacos may be seen.

Practical information
The best months to visit Península Valdés and Punta Tombo or Camarones are September to November, when all the animals can be seen establishing territories, mating, or giving birth. December to February are almost as good. Between March and July you are unlikely to see any marine wildlife.

There are several camp sites, but you should bring all food supplies with you. Water is scarce. Be prepared for the constant wind.

Los Alerces National Park

Sixty kilometres west of Esquel, this lesser known national park is famous for its ancient larch trees, glistening lakes, waterfalls and forest covered peaks rising to 2253 metres. Lake Futalaufquen, on the east side of the park, also contains fat trout, much sought after by fishing enthusiasts (season Nov 1 to April 15). The park, which covers 263,000 hectares, has a number of well marked trails, as well as several hotels (some specifically for fishing fanatics), camp sites and bungalows which can be hired. You can also make boat trips across the lakes. If you wish to fish you must get a permit. Maps can be obtained from the tourist office in Esquel which is in front of the bus station.

The park is best entered from Esquel, although you can also reach it from a separate entrance through Trevelin following the Río Futaleufú. However, the vast Futaleufú hydroelectric dam prevents you from going very far in to the park, and entry to Lago Situación is forbidden. Buses leave regularly from Esquel to Los Alerces or you can join a tour. If you want to fish, enquire at the Sol del Sur travel agency, 9 de Julio 1086. Incidentally, we also managed to change a few travellers cheques here on a Sunday — the only place in the whole of Patagonia that would take them.

"I spent four days camping here. To see the *alerce* trees you must go on a boat trip across Lago Menéndez ($20 from Esquel, $10 from Lago Verde) but these will only run if there are at least ten people. Camping is officially forbidden around Lago Verde. The trails marked on the park map are mostly fictitious — only the trails around the Administracíon are kept cleared. The only long trail is from Lago Futalaufquen west to Naufragio de Frey where there is a *refugio*.

"In summer there are daily buses through the park, but in April there were only two buses a week — on Wednesday and Sunday from Esquel and Tuesdays and Saturdays from Bariloche." (P. Frew)

Erik Nijland writes: 'We think this is a really wonderful park, especially when you are coming from southern Patagonia and are fed up with the thorn bush and the wide landscapes there. This will be your first really *green* area. There is perfect camping near the entrance of the park, near the village of Futalaufquen (Los Maítenes). It does not rain as much here as in Bariloche. An interesting three day walk in the park is the circuit around Cerro Alto and Cerro el Petizo, two peaks overlooking Lago Menendez and Lago Rivadavia in the northeastern section of the park.'

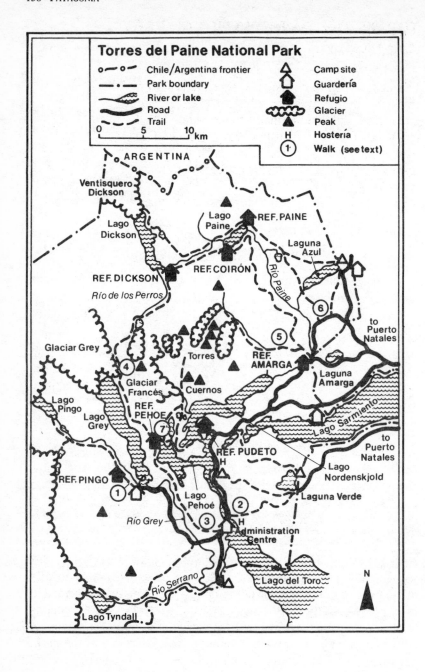

Torres del Paine National Park

○—○ ○ ○	Chile/Argentina frontier
—·—·—	Park boundary
~~	River or lake
===	Road
---	Trail

0 — 5 — 10 km

Camp site
Guardería
Refugio
Glacier
Peak
H Hostería
①· Walk (see text)

ARGENTINA

Ventisquero Dickson

Lago Dickson

Lago Paine

REF. PAINE

Laguna Azul

REF. DICKSON

REF. COIRÓN

Río de los Perros

Río Paine

⑥

⑤

to Puerto Natales

Glaciar Grey

④

Torres

REF. AMARGA

Laguna Amarga

Glaciar Francés

Cuernos

Lago Pingo

REF. PEHOE

Lago Grey

⑦

Lago Sarmiento

REF. PUDETO
H

to Puerto Natales

REF. PINGO

①

Lago Pehoé

②

H
Administration Centre

③

Río Grey

Lago Nordenskjold

Laguna Verde

Río Serrano

Lago del Toro

N

Lago Tyndall

TORRES DEL PAINE NATIONAL PARK

Of all the mountains I have seen in South America, the Paine massif remains my favourite. During our February visit we were blessed with freakishly perfect weather: a hot sun blazing from a cloudless sky, the normally fierce winds lulled to a gentle breeze, the bushes heavy with *calafate* berries and the meadows bright with foxgloves and ox-eye daisies. We had every reason to think we were in paradise.

The granite Paine towers thrust like giant fingers behind the Cuernos del Paine, an oddly shaped chunk of pinkish-white granite topped with crumbly sedimentary rock. Snow covered Paine Grande lies to the west. These mountains appear suddenly on the horizon after miles of flat, dry, windswept plain: an astonishing sight.

Various hikes can be done along the park's 250 kilometres of well marked trails, the most popular — justifiably — being the one to Lago and Glaciar Grey. This takes three or four days there and back, but a more ambitious hike of about eight days will take you right round the Paine massif to Lagos Grey, Dickson and Paine. There are also fine walks to Laguna Verde (two to three days there and back), Lago Pingo (two days each way) and to Laguna Azul and Refugio Paine (about five days there and back). The most amazing view is probably the close-up of the Paine towers from the glacial lake below. You will never forget it. All hikes are signposted with red or orange paint markings. Whichever you decide to do, allow plenty of time. Some people insist that three weeks is an absolute minimum in such a beautiful park, although this takes a fair bit of planning as you need to take most of your own food.

The park was established in 1959, under the name of Parque Nacional Lago Grey, covering an area of 5000 hectares. Before this shepherds grazed their flocks here, and their fires occasionally burned out of control, devastating large areas near Lagos Paine and Grey. The landscape still bears the scars. In 1962, 25,000 hectares were added, and the name was changed. It is said that a woman climber named Paine gave her name to the massif and to the park, but since *payne* is also an Indian word for blue — apt to describe the magnificent turquoise of many of the park's lakes — that may be the origin.

Numbers visiting the park have increased dramatically over recent years, most of them foreigners. As a result many of the *refugios* have taken a battering and several have been vandalized or destroyed by fires, deliberate or accidental. Fire is a permanent hazard so you need to take special care in putting out fires properly and making sure cigarette ends are extinguished.

There is a $10 entrance fee. The wardens are friendly and helpful, so do not hesitate to ask for information or advice. If you want to identify some of the birds or plants you have seen, the Administration Centre has a moderately informative exhibition of posters. It has no books however, so serious botanists/zoologists should buy their own before leaving home or in Buenos Aires or Santiago. For climbing information see page 168.

Getting there

The park entrance is 150 kilometres north of Puerto Natales, in the province of Magallanes. In season, Servitur and San Cayetano run daily bus services from Puerto Natales into the park, departing 6.30am and 7.00am and arriving three and a half hours later at the Administration Centre. (Times subject to change.) The return buses leave at 12.00pm and 1.00pm. Be sure to book your ticket into the park as soon as you get to Puerto Natales as it gets full in high season. Patrick Symington reports that he was able to arrange on his return to be dropped off at Cerro Castillo where, by prior arrangement, he picked up a minibus to Calafate on the same day.

When you arrive there are several possible places to get off. If you want to start the hikes to Laguna Azul, Laguna Amarga or the Torres del Paine circuit (anticlockwise), you should get out at the *portería* at the entrance next to Lago Sarmiento. Otherwise you could stop at Refugio Pudeto, next to the Guardería Pehoé, 18 kilometres before the Administration Centre, or at the Río Pehoé camp site, ten kilometres before the Centre. You will have to pay a fee of $8 per tent here since it is a privately run site, but you have the use of toilets, showers, tables and chairs.

If you have been roughing it for a while you may feel like splashing out on a room in the expensive Hostería Pehoé, perched on a small island on Lago Pehoé 13 kilometres north of the Administration Centre. You enjoy magnificent views of the Cuernos del Paine and the laundry will leave your clothes pristine, but you may prefer to save this treat for when you have completed the circuit. Cheaper accommodation is available at the more basic Posada Río Serrano, 200 yards from the Administration on the shores of Lago Toro. This has a well stocked but extremely pricey shop where you can buy food and drink (but not bread) and a quaint old fashioned bar/restaurant with white starched tablecloths where bow-tied tight-lipped waiters will serve you a hot chocolate or bacon and eggs. Bookings for the Posada or the Hostería can be made in Puerto Natales at Via Arturo Prat 270 (tel 355); in Punta Arenas at Turismo Pehoé, 21 de Mayo 1464 (tel 224506 or 224223); in Santiago at Nataniel 31, oficina 68 (tel 718709 or 6988287).

If the above two hotels are outside your budget, try either Hostería Las Torres or Refugio Lago Toro (need sleeping bag and mat).

Walks in the Park (keyed to the map)
by Christine and John Myerscough and Claire Hargreaves, updated by Patrick Symington, Simon Elms

1. Lago Pingo
The walk starts on the southern shore of Lago Grey. In summer you can probably get here from the Administration Centre by hitching a lift along the road on one of the tour buses. The road ends at a *guardería*. Take the trail which begins in front of the *guardería* and follows the river northwestwards. You soon reach Refugio Pingo, a nice *refugio* with two beds and a stove. The path from here is well marked. About five hours later you come to the former site of a hut and a *refugio*. They no longer exist but it is a good spot to camp. Alternatively you can continue another six hours upriver to the southern shores of Lago Pingo. You can camp anywhere but probably the best place is to your left near a big waterfall. From here you can admire the thousands of icebergs which have calved from the magnificent Ventisquero Pingo at the northern end of the lake and float eerily in its milky waters.

On your way back you can make a diversion about four kilometres before reaching the Administration Centre by following a 17-kilometre trail southwestwards to Lago Tyndall, another meltwater lake fed by an arm of the huge Ventisquero Geikie.

NOTE: Simon Elms reports that Lago Pingo is inaccessible as the bridge a couple of hundred metres past Refugio Zapata has fallen down and the river is too deep to ford. It may be possible to follow the river to its source — a small lake southwest of the Refugio. Or the bridge may have been rebuilt by the time you read this.

2. Laguna Verde
This walk is less trodden than many of the others in the park. Perhaps because of this, it offers one of the best collections of

wildlife in the whole park and you are almost certain to mingle with guanacos, rheas, foxes and Patagonian hares.

From the Administration Centre follow the main road north for two kilometres then turn right along the trail signposted Laguna Verde. About four hours later you will reach a *guardería* on the southern shore of Laguna Verde and a little further on an official camp site. The Laguna can also be reached by a trail going almost due east from the Río Pehoé camp site with the Cuernos behind you. This also takes four to five hours.

Leave Laguna Verde by the path which runs along the eastern side then leads northwest for 25 kilometres. When you reach the main road again (about six hours after leaving the lake), turn left and walk the few kilometres to Refugio Pudeto. While here you may like to visit the Salto Grande, an impressive waterfall where the waters of Lago Nordenskjold spill into Lago Pehoé. A bridge once linked the two sides and you could go this way to Lago Grey. Now it is no more than a rusty ruin and you will have to walk the 16 kilometres to the Administration Centre, unless you manage to catch the incoming bus or hitch a lift.

3. Lago Grey

Starting from the Administration Centre head west across the windswept golden grasslands from where you can enjoy magnificent views of the black-capped Cuernos. After about one and a half hours the well marked path veers north and follows the eastern banks of the milky Río Grey. Cutting across a strip of land you come to the southern shores of Lago Pehoé, a fairy-tale lake in whose turquoise waters you see reflections of the distant peaks. The path winds along the western shore then at the northern end dips down into a lush flat bottomed valley where you will find Refugio Pehoé. From the Administration Centre to Refugio Pehoé should take around four and a half hours. But there is a ferry. See page 168.

The *refugio* is one of the most scenically situated in the park. Operation Raleigh rebuilt it in 1990 and it is now one of the largest and nicest in the park, except we have received reports that it leaks. Alternatively, you may prefer to pitch your tent somewhere on the grassy plain on the lakeside where you can listen to the waves lapping onto the shore. Try to find a sheltered spot as the winds are often ferocious.

From Refugio Pehoé you can make a day trip up to the Glaciar Francés and Campamento Británico which nestles beside the Cuernos. This is described later in this section.

To continue to Glaciar Grey follow the well marked path going north which climbs up to a small secluded lake. Soon you emerge high above the eastern shore of Lago Grey where you enjoy fabulous views. Below, icebergs jam the southern end of Lago Grey while ahead the huge Glaciar Grey sprawls into infinity. Two or three hours later you drop down a muddy path into a leafy clearing, formerly the site of a *refugio* which was burned down and is now home to hordes of chattering parakeets. Just the toilet remains. This is an idyllic place to camp and there are plenty of fat blackcurrants for dessert. From here it is a few minutes to the snout of the glacier and you can explore the eerie blue ice caves or climb onto the snout. The whole walk from Refugio Pehoé should take around three hours. From Glaciar Grey you must either retrace your steps or continue on to Lago Dickson by the route described below.

4. The Torres del Paine circuit

This walk, which takes you to the remotest part of the park above Glaciar Grey and around Lagos Dickson and Paine, is undoubtedly the hardest. But it is also the most rewarding, with its perfect combination of tough mountain slogs and lazy strolls through daisy filled meadows. Unfortunately on the fourth day we woke up to find that the quiet pattering on our tent was not rain but snow. So be warned! The circuit can be walked clockwise or anti-clockwise, depending whether you want the agony first or last, and opinions seem to be divided as to which way is best. If you walk it anti-clockwise — leaving the agony until last, but having the wind behind you — you should set out from the *portería* near Lago Sarmiento. We describe the hike in a clockwise direction starting from Glaciar Grey.

The trail branches right about 400 metres beyond the new *refugio* site near the head of Lago Grey. It is not easy to find, but look for a small cairn. Follow it through the forest which runs along the side of the glacier and soon you come to a camp site beside a clear fast running stream. Every now and then the path emerges from the trees and takes you across scree-filled gullies carved out by rivers which tumble down into the glacier. Crossing these is fairly hair-raising as the scree tends to shift, so you should tread carefully. In some gullies there are wire cables for you to hang onto.

The steep path through the forest is not easy either. When it rains the ground turns to mud and you spend much of the time skidding and clambering over giant tree trunks which seem to have fallen across the trail deliberately to obstruct your way. After about four hours you reach another camp site. The stream supplying water for this site is about 50 yards north. You should camp here if it is getting late as the next site is not for seven to eight hours. The path then emerges above the treeline and cairns guide you up rocky slopes to the John Sarner pass, which, at 1350 metres is the highest point of the circuit. The trail from the camp site to the pass should take about two and a half hours. Here your toils will be amply rewarded: below, Glaciar Grey appears as a rippling sea of blue ice which stretches as far the eye can see towards the Patagonian icefield. This was for us the highlight of the entire trek, marred only slightly by the fact that a snow blizzard was threatening to blow us off our feet.

Just over the pass, follow the cairns and orange markings down the rocky slopes. This is often snow covered so tread carefully. An hour or so later you will have to ford a fast running river that flows from your left and is painfully cold. The track continues down the far bank over shale rock. If you need to stop here, there is a pocket handkerchief-sized camping spot on a flat rocky ledge beside the river about ten minutes below the crossing. This is the only camping place for miles as the rest of the terrain is squelchy bog. If you have time, however, you should continue another couple of hours until you reach the forest where there is a nicely sheltered camp site.

Before you enter the forest, the walk is quite amazing with glaciers, waterfalls and mountains on all sides, and a glacial lake with icebergs like blobs of blue detergent. When you get into the forest you will have to cross a couple of river tributaries but if you are lucky there should be tree trunks across them. You soon pass a camp site and then join an old herder's track through a sombre forest where you are likely to hear and see flame-crested Magellanic woodpeckers tapping on the tree trunks.

About five to six hours after the glacial lake you reach Refugio Dickson on the southern shores of Lago Dickson. The corrugated iron *refugio* used to be the home of a shepherd and still has a cast-iron cooking range (although this is now largely useless and constitutes a major fire hazard because it backs directly onto the wall of the hut). You will also find messages in all languages left by walkers who trod before you. In the garden you can find gooseberries, planted by the original owner and ready to eat in March, and extra fat *calafate* berries.

To get to Lago Paine from the *refugio*, follow the trail up the hill to the south and across the scrubland beside the Río Paine. You will pass the ruins of a hut. The terrain is boggy here so be careful.

About four hours later you reach Refugio Coirón, in a gully by a little stream: just a roof really as the hut has no stove and just an earth floor and a few planks for a bed. Alternatively there are plenty of good camping places beside the river from where you have fabulous views of Cerro Stokes (2150 metres) and Paine Medio and Grande.

When you reach Lago Paine, the well marked path climbs up along its southern banks. (There used to be a fine wooden bridge just before the lake which allowed you to cross to the northern banks and continue to Refugio Paine and Laguna Azul but this has now gone so you have to stay south.) As you reach the northern end of the lake the trail bends right and follows the Río Paine south all the way to Refugio Amarga.

The walk from Refugio Coirón to Refugio Amarga takes between eight and twelve hours. We took a day and a half, however, and camped on the way, allowing ourselves plenty of time to laze in the buttercup-filled meadows beside the river and watch herds of guanaco leap over the hills.

From Refugio Amarga, you can continue along the path which takes you over a hill and down to the *guardería* on the main road and out of the park a couple of hours later.

However, if you have the time you are strongly recommended to take the side trip up to the Torres (5) which branches off to the right just before you reach Refugio Amarga. You can get there and back in a day so you could leave your pack at the *refugio*. You may want to camp at the *estancia* and make the return trip the next day ($5 per tent, mixed reports as to the friendliness of the owners of the *estancia*). In any case, there are fabulous views of the Torres. Just after the *estancia*, the path crosses Río Ascencio, which flows out of the towers, by way of a new bridge. The trail then climbs steeply up the lefthand side of the river into the ever narrowing valley, finally reaching a glacial lake in about four hours. Here you enjoy some of the best views in the whole park. Beware of the strong winds that whistle through the towers, however: a backpacker died after being blown off a rock ledge up here. If you want to camp nearer the towers there is a designated camp site about two hours from the *estancia*, before entering the forested area, or a higher one with the remains of some shacks, below the final scramble to the glacial lake at the foot of the towers.

Another alternative from Refugio Amarga is to visit Laguna Azul and the northern part of the park. The trip, described below, takes about five days there and back.

6. Laguna Azul and Refugio Paine

The northeastern part of the park seems to be the least visited and yet one of the most attractive, being less barren and wild than some of the western and central areas.

Follow the road which leads out of the park from Refugio Amarga. Fork left beside the houses at the park entrance and follow this road north along the eastern side of the Río Paine. About an hour from the *refugio* you pass a huge waterfall and then leave the river to climb northeast into a wooded valley. The trail eventually levels out into a wide flat-bottomed valley where rhea roam. Just before the road swings south, fork left along an old little-used track which is signposted to Laguna Azul. After climbing up through lush meadows you zigzag down once more and emerge at the southwestern end of Laguna Azul. This area enjoys a microclimate much milder than the rest of the park and the lake shores are thick with ox-eye daisies and buttercups and a haven for many types of birds. You could camp here.

It takes a further four to five hours to reach Refugio Paine on the northern shores of Lago Paine. Follow the track which leads northwest from Laguna Azul and past the curiously named Laguna Cebolla (Onion Lagoon). Your path will be joined by the track from the eastern end of Laguna Azul. You soon reach Refugio Paine, a comfortable, spacious hut with a good wood burning stove and plenty of gooseberries, redcurrants and rhubarb in the garden. We also found huge quantities of giant white puffballs in the surrounding meadows which, when fried with garlic, were delicious. This is an ideal place to linger a few days.

From here you can continue along the northern shores of the lake to Lago Dickson. The path becomes quite faint as it winds north towards Lago Dickson but can be picked up again where it passes between two large rock faces before emerging high above the lake. You can just about get to and from Lago Dickson in a day but two days would be better and there is an idyllic camp site beyond the rocky pass beside a small lake in the woods. It is possible to descend to the lake shore and walk to the glacier at the northern end.

On your return journey from Refugio Paine you could take a different route via the *guardería* and camp site at the eastern end of Laguna Azul. It is from here that a road may one day link the Torres del Paine with Los Glaciares National Park in Argentina, but so far the countries have failed to reach agreement on its construction.

7. Side trip to Glaciar Francés and Campamento Británico

From Refugio Pehoé, follow the path that winds east along the shores of Lago Pehoé and then veers north across country to the Cuernos del Paine. After passing a signpost you walk beside two small sapphire-blue lakes, then cross the Río Francés just below the snout of the Glaciar Francés. Continue up the moraine ridge on the far side of the river for another two hours and you will reach a climbing hut known as Campamento Británico. If the weather is clear this walk, which takes about four and a half hours each way, gives you excellent close-up views of the Cuernos. If the cloud is low it is not worth doing.

A further option, after visiting Glaciar Francés, is to make a circular walk by following the path which leads back along the eastern shores of the small lakes and along the route that used to lead to the bridge at Salto Grande. This crosses some magnificent rugged Scottish-style landscape and takes you to a lovely beach on the edge of Lago Nordenskjold. The disadvantage of this route is that the path is tough going and poorly marked and involves at least two icy river crossings.

Practical information

Distance/time   Lago Pingo: 28 kilometres and two days each way. Overnight camp necessary.

Laguna Verde: 40 kilometres and one day each way.

Lago Grey: Two days each way, though you might make it there and back in three.

Refugio Pehoé to Campamento Británico: One day.

Torres del Paine Circuit: You should allow at least a week, more if you intend to take the side trails into the Torres or the Cuernos. The trails are mostly easy and well marked, except for the sections indicated above.

Preparations   Although the shop in the Posada Río Serrano sells food and drink it is very expensive so you are advised to bring your food. You can buy most things from Puerto Natales. At least a week's supplies are necessary for the Torres del Paine circuit. Between late January and March you will be able to supplement this with *calafate* berries, blackcurrants and giant puffballs. If you have your own transport, petrol and a tyre repair service are available at the Posada Río Serrano.

The weather is almost certain to be cold and windy at least some of the time so bring a change of clothing and a thick sweater or down jacket. Completely waterproof anorak and overtrousers are essential. Sneakers are also useful for those river fordings, and, unless you are doing the circuit, you may prefer to hike in them as well. You can get by without a tent by staying in the *refugios* except for the circuit where you definitely need one.

If you want to avoid the rather boring walk from the administration centre towards Refugio Pehoe, a ferry crosses Lago Pehoe daily at 1pm from Refugio Pedeto to Refugio Pehoe. It returns at 4pm.

NOTE: If you decide to do the Torres del Paine circuit, it is vital to ask the *guardaparque* about the current state of the trail between Lago Grey and Lago Dickson. It is faint and difficult and the pass between the two may be closed by snow. Do not attempt this section alone, make sure you have plenty of food, and carry a compass.

Peninsular walk
Patrick Symington adds this half day walk for the spectacular views it affords. It explores the peninsula that projects into Lago Nordenskjold beyond the Salto Grande. "On a clear day this gives fantastic views of Glaciar Francés and the Cuernos. There are a number of trails on the peninsula which can be followed. It makes a nice change from the main trails, and is easy and accessible. We did it from the Hosteriá Pehoé."

Maps   The best map is the excellent 1:100,000 topographical map produced by Sociedad Turística Kaonikén which is widely available in Puerto Natales ($3), and in the park itself. It includes trails and walking times.

Climbing   CONAF, the Chilean forestry organization which manages the park, has laid down rules and requirements for those wishing to undertake climbs within the park's boundaries. A permit from DIFROL is essential. This should be applied for at least a month before reaching the park. It's best done through your Chilean embassy, but can be obtained directly from DIFROL by contacting Dirección Nacional de Fronteras y Límites del Astado, Bandera 52 (50 Piso), Santiago, Chile (tel 56 2 671 41110/fax 56 2 697 1909). When you have the permit, you must go to the park's Administrative Centre and pay 330,000 Chilean pesos or the US$ equivalent. You'll be given a contract and asked to read, and state that you've understood, a copy of the park's rules. The climbing fee includes entrance to the park, but you'll have to leave all your equipment at the entrance until your paperwork has been completed.

LOS GLACIARES NATIONAL PARK, ARGENTINA
By Clare Hargreaves, and John and Christine Myerscough

Los Glaciares National Park, covering more than 6000km² of southern Argentina, offers a remarkable combination of breathtaking glaciers, spectacular mountain ranges, vast emerald green lakes and rare plants and animals. To the south is the Perito Moreno glacier, which spills into Lago Argentino. Huge chunks of ice break off from its massive blue ice cliff and crash into the water, creating small tidal waves. To the north are the granite pinnacles of Mount Fitz Roy (or Chaltén) and Cerro Torre, whose sheer cliffs make them a challenge for any climber.

The main centre for exploring the national park is **Calafate** on the southeastern shores of Lago Argentino. The quaint town is really just a single dusty street but it has an easy-going atmosphere which makes it a pleasant base from which to visit the surrounding area. Food and hotel prices are high. Indeed, food items, already inflated by the cost of transporting them thousands of miles, can be double the price you would pay further north.

Note that in Calafate it may be impossible to change travellers cheques, even at the bank. You should carry plenty of dollar notes which can be changed at the bank, at a *casa de cambio* or in a shop.

Getting there
If you are coming from Ushuaia, the best and cheapest way of getting to Calafate is on a regular flight with LADE. This also stops at Río Gallegos. By travelling this way you get a tempting glimpse of the Fitz Roy pinnacles just before you land. Interlagos Turismo and Pingüino both run a daily bus from Río Gallegos to Calafate departing at 3.00pm and 4.00pm respectively. The journey across barren pampas takes four hours.

If you are coming from Chile, there are a number of operators in Puerto Natales that organize visits. In season, buses leave every morning from Puerto Natales. This route takes approximately seven hours and is really only used by tourists. Most of the 333km road is unsurfaced track across desert wastes. The road is really only used by tourists, so the bus is expensive ($35 plus). If you are coming from the Torres del Paine we have been told it is possible to arrange to be dropped off at Cerro Castillo and picked up by the bus to Calafate.

20: Los Claciares NP (160)

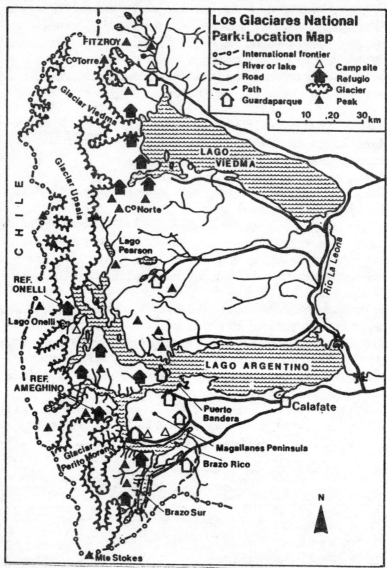

Getting out of Calafate can be more difficult. The best bet is probably the bus to Río Gallegos which leaves at 5.00am daily in summer (and at 9.15am in winter, three times a week). The journey takes five hours. Alternatively, take the LADE flight to Ushuaia or Río Grande or Río Gallegos. A warning however: these flights tend to be fully booked in high season and are often cancelled at the last minute because of high winds. There is no public transport along the road directly north to Perito Moreno and Esquel so if you are trying to get to either of these you will have to go via Río Gallegos and Comodoro Rivadavia unless you have a car. If you are thinking of hitching along this road (or to Río Gallegos for that matter) think again unless you fancy spending an entire week on a dusty roadside. In the four hours we waited, only one vehicle passed — and that was going to an *estancia* two kilometres up the road.

Where to stay in Calafate
Los Alamos, Gob. Moyano and Bustillo (tel 91144). New, well-equipped hotel, good food and service.
Hostería Kau Yatun near Ushuaia and Ruta Prov 11 (tel 91059). Comfortable old *estancia* house with restaurant and barbecue.
La Loma Roca and 15 de Febrero (tel 91016). Modern hotel with excellent view, garden, restaurant, tea room. Extra 14 economy rooms with private baths. Special rates for IYH members and people carrying this guide.
Hotel Amado, Av. Libertador (tel 91023). Centrally situated. Restaurant.
Hospedaje Belen Los Cauchos and Perito Moreno (tel 91028). Clean, warm, basic accommodation with hot water and cooking facilities.
Hospedaje Jorgito, Gob. Moyano (tel 91323). Clean accommodation with heating and hot water (breakfast extra). Often full.
Albergue del Glaciar On edge of town near road to Río Gallegos. One of the friendliest places on our whole trip.

Camping
Municipal camp site behind the YPF petrol station, two further sites without facilities en route to the glaciers, and one at Lago Roca with restaurant, showers, toilets and autocamping facilities.

Perito Moreno glacier
Along with the Iguazú Falls and Machu Picchu, Glaciar Moreno must rank as one of the most astonishing sights of South America. The glacier, named after the 19th century Argentine explorer Francisco Perito Moreno whose statue adorns the square of every Patagonian town, is unique in being one of the few glaciers that has been growing. Its vast blue ice front, one kilometre wide and nearly 50 metres above the surface of the lake, is a staggering spectacle. Its drama is further enhanced by the fact that every few minutes fairy-tale ice towers, the size of 20-storey buildings, crash into the water making a thunder so loud you could be under artillery bombardment.

One of the most fascinating features of the glacier is that its advancing wall of blue ice periodically cuts Lago Argentino in two by blocking the narrow stretch of lake known as the Canal de los Témpanos (Icebergs Channel). This prevents the natural drainage of Brazo Rico, the up-valley arm of Lago Argentino, causing its water level to rise as much as 36 metres above the level of the rest of the lake. Gradually the lake water hollows out a tunnel through the ice barrier until it finally collapses and the water in the Brazo Rico rushes through creating enormous waves. This used to happen every three to four years and last occured at the end of 1991 but not in such a spectacular manner. There are reports that due to global warming the glacier has stopped or slowed down its growing process and it is estimated the cycle will only recur every seven years.

Glaciar Moreno is 85 kilometres from Calafate and can be reached by car or, in summer, by minibus. All Calafate's travel companies run tours to the glacier, bookable one or two days before. Most leave around 9.00am, returning home at 5.00pm, giving you about three hours at the glacier (cost $25 excluding park entrance fee, $4). There are also more expensive tours of the glacier which include boat trips in front of the glacier and a walk over the top of the glacier. Take lunch as there is no food on sale near the glacier. We went with Lake Tours and were treated to a running commentary in Spanish, Italian and French. Los Glaciares bus company go there (tel 0902 91159) or if you are lucky you may be able to hitch an early morning lift on one of the trucks from the National Park office which is one of the last buildings on the main street as you head northwest out of town.

Undoubtedly the best means of experiencing the full mystery of Perito Moreno is to camp in the park. This way you can avoid the coachloads of camera-toting tourists who cram the glacier's viewing platforms in the day and you can enjoy it in peace in the evening sunshine when they have all gone home. There are two designated camp sites in the park, one 54 kilometres out of Calafate in a pleasant wooded area on the shores of Brazo Rico, the other seven kilometres before the glacier at Bahía Escondida. Permits can be bought from the *guardaparque* at the park entrance. Patrick Symington reports that there is a semi-official site closer to the glacier, just beyond the helicopter pad. No facilities are available and you will need to obtain permission from the *guardaparque*. There are also a number of *refugios* (see Location Map). For details enquire at the National Park office in Calafate. There is a *hostería* overlooking the lake and glacier, which has a restaurant and several log bungalows to sleep four. No cooking allowed in the cabins so take food to eat cold. In summer you will need to book well in advance.

If you can afford it, take the 12 minute helicopter flight which goes along the face of the glacier and up the crevasse valleys. Well worth the $40 it cost in 1990.

Upsala and Onelli glaciers

In summer you can take a boat to the magnificent glaciers on the northern end of Lago Argentino where you cruise among giant icebergs. The tour leaves Calafate at 6.30 am (boat leaves at 8.00am from Punta Bandera, 45 kilometres west of Calafate, if you you have your own transport). The boat takes you to the Upsala, Agassiz, Bolado, Onelli and Spegazzini glaciers and stops for lunch at Bahía Onelli where there is a restaurant. Because of the boat journey this tour is much more expensive than the trip to Perito Moreno: a tour starting in Calafate will cost around $80 including bus fares and park entry.

The park map shows the existence of several *refugios* on the far shores of Lago Argentino. It was suggested to us that we might like to be dropped off by one of the tour boats and be picked up again a few days later so we could visit some of the remote glaciers in these western fjords. We did not have time to follow up the idea, but you may like to ...

MOUNT FITZ ROY AND CERRO TORRE
Updated by John Pilkington and Graham Youdale, with Patrick Symington

The major attraction of the park for walkers is without doubt the mountain range on the northwest shores of Lago Viedma, 240 kilometres north of Calafate, which includes the granite pinnacles of Mount Fitz Roy (3441 metres) and Cerro Torre (3128 metres).

Francisco Moreno named Fitz Roy after Robert Fitzroy, the captain of the Beagle. But the Araucanian Indian tribes that once roamed Patagonia, who saw the mountain as a god, called it Chaltén which means 'god of smoke' because of its almost permanent veil of self-created mist. Indeed, until this century people believed the mountain was a volcano in eruption and it was only recently that this was proved untrue.

Because the Indians respected Chaltén they never sought to conquer it. In fact the first ascents of both Fitz Roy and Cerro Torre were made only recently. Two Italians, Terray and Magnone, were the first to climb Fitz Roy in 1952. The conquest of Cerro Torre —

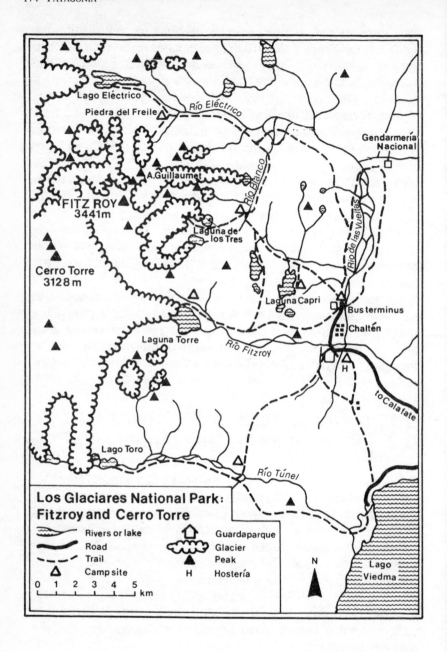

Los Glaciares National Park:
Fitzroy and Cerro Torre

≈≈≈ Rivers or lake
━━━ Road
- - - Trail
△   Camp site

Guardaparque
Glacier
▲ Peak
H Hostería

0 1 2 3 4 5
|__|__|__|__|__| km

N

once rated as unclimbable — is the subject of controversy. An Italian named Maestre claimed to have reached the summit in 1959. But his companion, Egger, was killed during the descent and Maestre was later found in a bad state and unable to recall much of the climb. He returned in 1970 with three companions but his use of a compressor driven drill to put up bolts as footholds drew storms of protest. The first ascent is usually credited to another group of Italians, led by Casimiro Ferrari, who climbed Cerro Torre in 1974.

To enjoy these mountains fully you will need at least five days — more if the weather is fine and you fancy a day or two to relax.

Getting there

Interlagos Turismo run a daily bus called Los Glaciares which leaves at 7.00am, arrives around midday and returns around 3.30pm. Chaltén Patagonia operate a similar service: the cost for both companies is $35 return. As it enters the park the bus stops at the Administration Centre where walkers and climbers must get a permit and declare how long they intend to stay. There is a good map on display here, but it is not for sale. The best map can be bought in Calafate at a small printers some 200m past the National Parks Office (which also publishes a reasonable map). We have received reports that walkers no longer need to register, nevertheless anyone attempting any serious walking in this area would be well advised to do so.

If you do not have camping gear there are two places to stay, both of which the bus passes on its way into the park. Very basic accommodation can be found at the Lago Desierto (around $15 a night). Alternatively you can stay at the more expensive Estancia La Quinta (three kilometres from Chaltén). Nearby are two small grocery stores selling basic provisions. There is a free camp site about one kilometre further on near the spot where the bus terminates.

Directions

The bus will drop you at the Guardería Madsen beside the fast-running Río de las Vueltas. From here you have a choice of two main walks with some route variations. You can either take the righthand path up through the woods towards Río Blanco Base Camp at the foot of Fitz Roy's east face and Lago Eléctrico to the north. Or you can take the lefthand trail along the Río Fitz Roy to Laguna Torre from where you get a view (if you are lucky) of

Cerro Torre. Since most people go to Fitz Roy first, we start with this hike.

Mount Fitz Roy

The path to Río Blanco starts right of a wooden hut and takes you steeply through a wood in a northwesterly direction. About an hour later you emerge into the open and walk along a ridge from where you have your first close-up view of the spires of Mount Fitz Roy. Soon you come to a sign to Laguna Capri. This is well worth a visit but we saved it until later on. The path now drops down into the magnificent valley of the Chorrillo del Salto which you follow until you reach the wide Río Blanco. There is a camp site in the woods this side of the river which few people seem to know about. The main camp site is the other side so you will have to cross using stepping stones or boulders (depending on the state of the river). You will reach the Río Blanco camp site 15 minutes later, hidden in the trees. Unfortunately the site is fairly scruffy due to the fact that it is used as a long-term base camp by large groups of climbers. They have built several crude *refugios* where they store equipment, but these are not for general use. We found a quiet spot to camp in the woods beside a tiny stream. The walk from the bus terminus to Río Blanco takes two to three hours.

From Río Blanco it is well worth making a side trip to the magnificent emerald green lake at the foot of the Fitz Roy pinnacles called Laguna de los Tres. This is a straightforward one-hour climb up a rocky path which starts at the left of the camp site and takes you to the lip of the corrie which contains Laguna de los Tres. Be careful of your footing as there is a lot of shifting scree at the top. From a point to the left of the lake you can also look down on the magnificent Laguna Sucia, often dotted with icebergs. From Laguna de los Tres it is worth continuing south to Laguna Sucia. Simon Elms suggests climbing down beside the two streams which leave Laguna de los Tres. The righthand stream is easier as the lefthand one becomes a waterfall. It took Simon about an hour to descend and 'scared the hell out of me'. He also suggests that you can walk back to the Río Blanco by following the north bank of the stream that leaves Laguna Sucia, although it is a 'bit of a scramble'.

Once you are back at Río Blanco it is well worth continuing to another camp site at the foot of the north face of Fitz Roy, known as Piedra del Freile. From here you can visit the quaintly named Lago Eléctrico or make a side trip up to Fitz Roy. The ten kilometre walk to Piedra del Freile takes about five and a half hours. Follow the path which heads north along the right bank of the Río Blanco. After about two hours the path crosses the river and heads northwest through beautiful deciduous woodland and daisy-filled meadows. An hour or so after leaving the Río Blanco you should meet another well marked path from the right which is signposted to La Florida police station. Ignore this and continue left. Shortly afterwards you cross a stream and wind your way up through the woods beside the Río Eléctrico until you reach a lush wide valley. Here you will spot Refugio Los Troncos sheltered from the icy winds coming off the glaciers at the head of the valley by a huge lump of rock which gives the location its name, Piedra del Freile. This *refugio* is privately run and the owner charges $10 a night or $5 to camp. We have had mixed reports as to his character and nature. He also reportedly sells drinks and some food, but this is, not suprisingly, very expensive, given he has to carry it in. Try to find a camp site with a bit of shelter as the winds can be vicious.

From Piedra del Freile you can make the short but steep climb up to the foot of the north face of Fitz Roy. The path starts on the lefthand side of the valley and climbs up the righthand side of the stream which tumbles down from the mountain. The trail ends at a scree-filled basin below A Guillaumet (2593 metres, 2579 metres or 2503 metres depending on which map you believe). Half a day should be sufficient to get there and back.

An alternative route back from Río Blanco/Río Electrico: either from the Río Blanco path or from the path to the *gendarmería*, cross the Río Blanco. Most people cross near the point where the Piedra del Freile route leaves the river; pick your way across boulders and through riverside woods, following the right bank of the Río Blanco to where it passes between a small wooded hill on the left and the main hillside on the right. Here pick up a path along the river bed which is marked by red-spotted stones. Opposite the summit of the wooded hill on the left the path turns away from the river, passes through a gate in an electric fence, and winds gradually upwards into the hills. One and a half hours after leaving Río Blanco you crest a small summit, drop down to a stream, before climbing to a second high point beyond which Laguna Polo nestles in a basin surrounded by trees. Descending from the lagoon you will reach the valley road within a half hour. From here it is an hour's slog to Chaltén.

Cerro Torre

The simplest way to get to Cerro Torre is to start from the bus terminus and to follow the well marked track along the valley of the Río Fitz Roy as far as Laguna Torre. However, if you are coming from Piedra del Freile you can avoid going all the way back by cutting across the area around Laguna Capri south of Río Blanco. We describe how to reach Cerro Torre this way, returning along the valley.

Retrace your steps from Río Blanco towards Chaltén. After about 15 minutes, where the trail crosses the Chorrillo del Salto, leave it and turn south, keeping to the higher ground to the left of a shallow valley which leads up to the two lakes known as Madre y Hija (mother and daughter). Between these is a pleasant place to camp. Keep left of both lakes, then cross to the right of a smaller lake just visible from the trail. From here the path becomes more distinct, and is marked here and there by strips of red cloth tied to sticks and branches. Eventually you come out on the main path up the Fitz Roy valley. The walk from the Río Blanco crossing to here takes about three and a half hours.

The path to Cerro Torre takes you across a wide flat area of shrubs and bushes and then enters woods. About 200 metres into the woods, the path branches. The lefthand branch takes you to Campamento Base de Jim Bridwell by the lake and the righthand branch climbs steeply up onto a huge moraine ridge which encloses Laguna Torre. There is a camp site beside the lake. The Campamento de Jim Bridwell from all accounts is more popular and more pleasant. From either you will see the Ventisquero Grande which feeds the lake, and, if you are lucky, the impressive rock towers of Cerro Torre, Torre Egger and Cerro Stanhardt. Do not be surprised, however, if you see nothing at all: Cerro Torre is notorious for hiding in cloud. We met one photographer who had waited three days for it to emerge but never saw it. From Laguna Torre it is possible to scramble along the scree beside Ventisquero Grande as far as the base of Cerro Torre. The walk along the main path to the bus terminus will take around three hours.

If you are heading for Río Blanco from Laguna Torre, descend the Río Fitz Roy valley for about an hour, and look out for the trail ten metres below a sign reminding you to pack out your rubbish. You will have to concentrate more if the sign has been removed: after your path touches the bank of the Río Fitz Roy, you cross a flat meadow for 15 minutes before climbing gently around the end of a ridge. 40 metres beyond the high point you will see the path to the left, faint at first, then becoming clearer as it enters the woodland.

Lago Toro

One other possible hike is the two to three day walk to Lago Toro, south of the administration area. You may be able to sleep in the small *puesto* en route, but ask the *guardaparques* about this before leaving. You can return a slightly different way by forking right before the path crosses back to the northern side of Río Túnel. We understand there is a path on the south side of the river but you may find it difficult to cross the river. Try at either the *puesto* or on the shores of Lago Viedma. If you are able to cross, it saves returning to the administration centre on the same path.

Practical information

Time/rating   You will need five to six days to do all the walks. The best time to go is December to March.

Preparations   As in the Torres del Paine, you should be prepared for all weathers. Waterproofs and warm clothing are essential. Although the walking is fairly easy, it is advisable to wear walking boots for the bits across scree.

Maps   There is a new topographical map of the area (1:50,000). It was published in 1992 by Zaiger & Urruty and is widely available in Calafate and has been approved by the IGM. It shows all of the walks, with the exception of the Lago Toro walk. Avoid buying any older maps as they are notoriously unreliable.

180

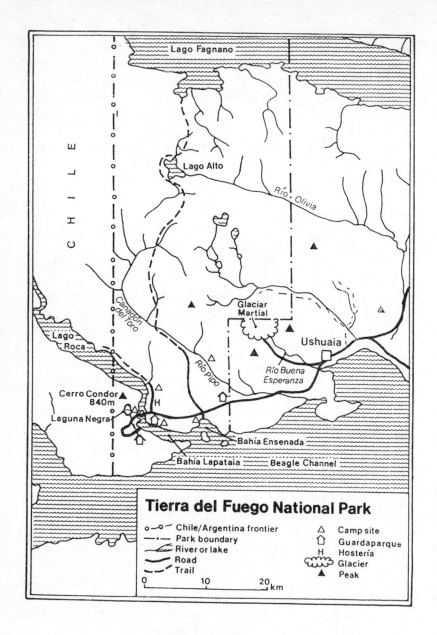

Tierra del Fuego National Park

o—o Chile/Argentina frontier
—·—· Park boundary
River or lake
Road
Trail

0   10   20 km

△ Camp site
⌂ Guardaparque
H Hostería
Glacier
▲ Peak

Lago Fagnano
Lago Alto
Río Olivia
CHILE
Cañadón del Toro
Glaciar Martial
Ushuaia
Lago Roca
Río Pipo
Cerro Condor 840m
Río Buena Esperanza
Laguna Negra
H
Bahía Ensenada
Bahía Lapataia — Beagle Channel

Chapter Twelve

Tierra del Fuego

To the south we had a scene of savage magnificence, well becoming Tierra del Fuego. There was a degree of mysterious grandeur in mountain behind mountain, with the deep intervening valleys, all covered by one thick, dusky mass of forest. The atmosphere, likewise, in this climate, where gale succeeds gale, with rain, hail, and sleet, seems blacker than anywhere else. In the Strait of Magellan, looking due southward from Port Famine, the distant channels between the mountains appeared from their gloominess to lead beyond the confines of this world.
Charles Darwin, *The Voyage of the Beagle*, 17 December 1832.

Introduction
When, in 1520, the Portuguese explorer Ferdinand de Magellan reached the great rugged island at the tip of America, he observed the black smoke from the fires lit by the local Indians to warn each other that a stranger had been sighted. He called it Tierra del Humo, Land of Smoke. His patron, Charles V of Spain, reasoning that there could be no smoke without fire, renamed the island Tierra del Fuego, Land of Fire.

Around 300 years later, racked with seasickness after the stormy voyage round Cape San Diego on the island's southeast tip, Fitzroy anchored the Beagle a few miles along the coast in the Bay of Good Success. Here he made his first acquaintance with the island's 'savages' — native Yahgan Indians, who were later virtually wiped out by measles and tuberculosis imported by white settlers (see Box on page 184).

Today there are no 'pure blooded' Indians. And the only fires burning are those that flicker from the oil fields, the island's main industry apart from tourism and sheep farming.

Given its proximity to the treacherous shipwreck-studded rocks of Cape Horn, 70 miles south, Tierra del Fuego comes as a pleasant surprise if you want to walk. The north of the island, with a similar climate and landscape to the Patagonian plains, contrasts with the beautiful southern part where the mighty Andes finally dive into the sea and jagged snow-covered peaks overlook forests of southern beech and flower-studded meadows. Summer can be almost warm.

For experienced mountaineers, some of the most beautiful peaks in South America are to be found in this area, including the twin-summited Monte Sarmiento, accessible from Puerto Williams and named by early navigators of the Magellan Straits.

Much of Tierra del Fuego has only recently been occupied and is given over to sheep farming. The *estancias* are vast, usually over 10,000 acres, and virtually self-sufficient, with a kitchen garden, carpenters' shop and blacksmith.

Tierra del Fuego is divided more or less equally between Chile and Argentina. The Argentine part is more developed, and its administrative centre, Ushuaia, is the island's largest settlement. The chief town on the Chilean side is Porvenir from where you can get a ferry to Punta Arenas. Ushuaia, which overlooks the emerald waters of the Beagle Channel, still boasts of being the southernmost city in the world, but the southernmost settlement is the Chilean naval base of Puerto Williams which lies across the strait on the island of Navarino. The long-running border dispute between the two countries meant that you used not to be able to cross from one town to the other for longer than a day. We understand there are no longer any restrictions.

Ushuaia, which in the tongue of the native inhabitants means 'inner harbour to westward', has been aptly described as a cross between Fort William in Scotland and an Austrian ski resort. The city consists of modern, concrete houses sprawled over the hills overlooking the Beagle Channel. In bizarre contrast, the main street is lined with glossy duty free shops parading imported chocolates, hi-fis, clothes, shoes and liquor.

Because of its tax free status and higher wages, Ushuaia has attracted many Argentines in search of wealth and the city has become something of a boom town. It is also a popular destination for Argentine holidaymakers. Hotels, which are expensive anyway, tend to be packed. The best bet is to stay in one of the numerous reasonably priced *pensiones* (bookable through the Tourist Office) or to camp.

Several tour operators run walking trips into Tierra del Fuego National Park and to Mount Olivia to the east. Try Caminante or Kilak Expeditions which has an office on Rivadavia between Maipu and San Martín.

There is a good camp site, Camping Río Tristen, which is part of the Haruwen winter sports centre, 19 miles to the east of the city on RN3. The site has baths, showers, electric lighting, a dining room, campfire facilities with tables and chairs, and five miles of signposted trekking paths. The daily fee is US$5 for a tent with two occupants. The site can be reached by a regular bus service from Ushuaia, where Haruwen has an office at San Martín 788 L.36 (tel/fax 24058).

Getting there
The easiest and cheapest way to reach Ushuaia from Calafate or Río Gallegos is to fly with LADE (heavily booked in summer). Aerolíneas Argentinas fly from Río Gallegos. Aerolíneas Argentinas also run a weekly flight to Punta Arenas (but check this still runs). Buses run from Río Grande to Ushuaia daily and stop on the way at the ACA *hostería* on the shores of Lago Fagnano.

If you are coming from Chile, two ferries cross the Magellan Strait: one between Punta Arenas and the sleepy port of Porvenir (Wednesdays, Fridays, Saturdays and Sundays), the second between the port 27km from Punta Delgada and Punta Espora (times vary according to the tides). The whole journey takes about seven and a half hours.

TIERRA DEL FUEGO NATIONAL PARK
updated by Christine and John Myerscough

Ten kilometres west of Ushuaia, along the main road beside the Beagle Channel, is the entrance to Tierra del Fuego National Park. This is a beautiful area covering 63,000 hectares and combining the clear blue lakes and snow-capped mountains of the Cordón del Toro with the peaceful shores of Lago Roca and Bahía Lapataia. Unfortunately there are few established trails within the park but it is still well worth exploring. There are a number of designated camp sites with fireplaces and fresh water which are free, except for the  main one at Lago Roca which is about $10 per tent. There is a park entrance fee of $4. Permission to camp and fish in the area should be obtained from the *guardaparque* at the park entrance.

In summer, a number of bus operators run buses to Lago Roca in the park. Turismo Pasarela (Fadul 40, tel 21735) run a minibus four times a day. Likewise, Caminante operate a minibus service a couple of times a day. The fare is $15 return.

THE FUEGIAN INDIANS
by Clare Hargreaves

> The next day we ... came to a more inhabited district. Few if any of these natives could ever have seen a white man: certainly nothing could exceed their astonishment at the apparition of the four boats. Fires were lighted on every point (hence the name of Tierra del Fuego), both to attract our attention and to spread far and wide the news. Some of the men ran for miles along the shore. I shall never forget how wild and savage one group appeared. Suddenly four or five men came to the edge of an overhanging cliff: they were absolutely naked, and their long hair streamed about their faces; they held rugged staffs in their hands, and, springing from the ground, they waved their arms around their heads, and sent forth the most hideous yells.
>
> It was as easy to please as it was to satisfy these savages. Young and old, men and children, never ceased repeating the word 'yammerschooner', which means 'give me'. After pointing to almost every object one after the other, even to the buttons on our coats, and saying their favourite word in as many intonations as possible, they would then use it in a neuter sense, and vacantly repeat 'yammerschooner.' After yammerschoonering for any article very eagerly, they would point to their young women or little children, as much as to say, 'If you will not give it me, surely you will to such as these.'
>
> Charles Darwin, Diary 20 January 1833.

Little more than a century ago, the only inhabitants of Tierra del Fuego were Indians. These belonged to four tribes, each with their own language and customs: the Ona, the Alacaloof, the Yahgan and the Aush (see box on next page). Living in wigwams, they survived by hunting guanaco with bows, arrows and slings and fishing in bark canoes. Contrary to what Darwin believed, human flesh never formed part of their diet: their strict code of customs forbade this. Darwin also did the Indians a gross injustice by describing their language as "hideous yells." The language of one of the tribes, the Yahgans, was actually far richer than English or Spanish, with a vocabulary of no fewer than 32,000 words and inflections.

Incredibly hardy, the Indians could go naked even when it was snowing and withstand the toughest physical rigours. Tragically, however, they had no resistance to white men's diseases. With the arrival in 1871 of the first white colonists — first missionaries, then farmers and bureaucrats — hundreds died of measles. More horrific still, others met their deaths at the hands of greedy white settlers who saw the Indians as troublesome vermin and offered a pound a head for every one killed. By 1947, of the seven to nine thousand Indians who had inhabited this bleak island when Darwin visited, there were less than 150 left. Today there are none.

THE FUEGIAN TRIBES

The Ona

These inhabited the remote interior of the main island and its northern and eastern coasts. The only weapons used by the Ona were bows and arrows, and they lived almost entirely on guanaco meat. They clothed themselves in the skins of these animals as well as using them for their shelters.

The Alacaloof

Natural adventurers, the Alacaloof lived on the western parts of the archipelago and survived by fishing in bark canoes. They lived almost entirely on birds, seal, fish and limpets. They were also dexterous in the use of bows and arrows, spears and slings.

The Yahgan

These were the southernmost inhabitants of the earth. Their territory extended from Desolation Bay, along the southern coast of the main island as far as Spaniard Harbour (including Ushuaia) and took in all the southern islands down as far as Cape Horn. Work was fairly divided between the sexes. The men gathered fuel and fungi, while the women cooked, fetched water, paddled canoes and fished. Fish, seals, limpets, birds and crabs were the main diet. Because of the lack of beaches, the women had to swim like dogs through thick seaweed — in winter coated in frost — onto which they moored their canoes.

The Aush

The Aush (or Eastern Ona) lived on the boggy southeastern tip of the main island. They lived off hunting and fishing.

Cañadón del Toro and Río Pipo

NOTE: Readers should check with the *guaradapaque* before attempting this hike. Recent reports are that it has become overgrown and impassable.

About one and a half kilometres from the *guardaparque* a road branches right off the main road and takes you to within half a kilometre of the Cañadón del Toro which meets the Río Pipo. Near the end of the road is a (free) camp site with fireplaces and fresh water provided by the river. After the waterfall the road continues through woodland and past *turberas* (peat bogs). Interesting features also include the old prison railway whose rotting sleepers still remain and Indian relics such as forked logging drags for hauling logs out. To relieve the monotony of the road you could follow the railway which runs parallel.

A good hike from this camp site is the walk along the old trail which eventually leads to Lago Fagnano. Around 200 metres beyond the gate at the end of the road follow the jeep track that branches off left. This passes through woodland for about two kilometres, then enters an open meadow where there are signs of peat digging. The track eventually dwindles into a rather overgrown footpath. About two kilometres on you reach the ruins of a log cabin, but beyond this point there are only animal paths. The *guardaparque* says the trail which is marked on the map from here to Lago Fagnano no longer exists. Certainly if you wish to try it, you should take equipment, supplies and energy for several days' bushwhacking.

Bahía Ensenada
One and a half kilometres into the park you can also take the road which forks left and leads to the Bahía Ensenada. Just before the bay is another camp site with fireplaces and fresh water. The bay has a small pier from where you have good views over the Beagle Channel to Navarino and Hoste islands. Mussels can be collected along the eastern headland at low tide. Behind the camp site you will also see a collection of dams and lakes created by beavers, recently introduced from Canada. You can walk along the coast in either direction, but the hike to the west is very tough going and suitable only for experienced walkers. It takes about six hours to reach the main road and *guardería*.

Lago Roca and Cerro Cóndor
Another scenic camp site is on the shores of Lago Roca. To get there take the road which branches right off the main road about eight kilometres into the park. This leads to Hostería Alukush, which has a small store where you can buy supplies, and beyond, the Lago Roca camp site. The site — where you will have to pay — gets very crowded in summer so is best visited out of season.

One and a half kilometres west of the road junction just beyond the police post is another designated camp site (free and without facilities) which makes a good base from which to climb Cerro Cóndor (840 metres). There is no marked trail up the mountain, which looks very Scottish. Despite what the *guardaparques* tell you, the climb is nonetheless possible. The best way up is to follow the road across the bridge over the Río Lapataia and take the path to

Laguna Negra. A noticeboard here explains how the peat bogs around the lake are formed. Skirt west round the southern end of the lake, keeping to the high ground, out of the peat bog, and cross the small exit stream. Patrick Symington reports that the route is now marked but you would be well advised to take a compass bearing on the summit before entering the trees and follow this as best you can. After a two hour climb through the forest you emerge onto grassy slopes. It is another one and a half hours to the scree summit from which there are tremendous views. To the west you can see the snow covered peaks of the Darwin Range, below lie the glistening waters of the Beagle Channel, and beyond that the land breaks up into a jigsaw of islands, rounded off by the infamous Cape Horn.

Bahía Lapataia

Thirteen kilometres into the park the road ends at the scenic Bahía Lapataia. Shortly after the road crosses the Río Lapataia, a path (signposted to Sendero Ilustriva Los Castores) cuts through the woods, allowing you to avoid the last four kilometres of road. Several trails lead off this to delightful spots offering excellent birdwatching. In summer a huge catamaran picks up and sets down tourists at the bay as part of a tour from Ushuaia.

From Lapataia, Patrick Frew recommends hiking along the ridge between Bahía Lapataia and the Beagle Channel to the peak, Cerro Pirámide, on the Chilean border. This walk is known locally as the Balcones de Lapataia.

Begin the walk by following the trail along the shore of Bahía Lapataia. The trail leads to a smaller path which begins to rise. Near the top of this rise the path splits. Take the west path which involves a scramble up to the right of the cliffs above you. At the top you emerge in open woodland. You will pass by a beaver lake in an unlikely position by the col separating Cerros Cuchillo and Pirámide. It is a bit of a steep scramble down to the col and up to the broad Cerro Pirámide. Take care here as it can be quite dangerous. Return to Bahía Lapataia by the same route.

Practical information

Time/rating These are easy hikes but they should not be rushed. Allow two or three days in the National Park.

Preparations This is an area which is often buffeted by strong winds. Bring adequate protection, and make sure your tent can stand up to these conditions. The ground is likely to be boggy, so you may prefer to keep your boots dry by hiking in sneakers.

Maps The *guardaparque* at the entrance to Tierra del Fuego National Park will give you a photocopy map of the park and surrounding area. This is woefully inadequate for walking, however. A really beautiful map of all Tierra del Fuego has been published by Natalie Goodall in conjunction with her book on the island (see *Bibliography*). This can be bought in Ushuaia.

GARIBALDI PASS

An interesting walk to the north of Ushuaia, offering great views, is described by Simon Elms: 'I stopped off here on my way to Río Grande. The pass is an hour from Ushuaia and there are two buses a day, at 12.00 and 19.00, so I had seven hours for sightseeing before flagging down the evening bus at no extra cost. From the road you get a great view across Lagos Escondido and Fagnano to the north. For views south, along a huge mountain valley, you need to climb the ridge or spur to the west of the pass. From the pass a 4WD track leads up to a little saddle only a hundred metres from the main road to the west. From the saddle, head into the trees on the side of the spur. It is easy to pick up the path which is marked by spots or red paint on trees. The path appears to head straight up through the trees towards the ridge-line, but it actually sidles along the south flank of the spur and you emerge high up on the ridge after about 45 minutes. At one point the red markers peter out: remember that you're not heading straight up the slope but along the flank of the spur. There are great views to the south.

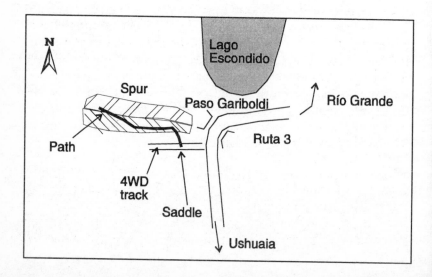

ESTANCIA HARBERTON:
THE UTTERMOST PART OF THE EARTH

Coming into Harberton from the land side, you could mistake it for a big estate in the Scottish Highlands, with its sheep fences, sturdy gates and peat-brown trout streams. The house, imported long ago from England, was of corrugated iron, painted white, with green windows and a soft red roof. Inside, it retained the solid mahogany furniture, the plumbing and the upright presence of a Victorian parsonage.
Bruce Chatwin, *In Patagonia.*

Anyone interested in the history of the island's Indian inhabitants — and their subsequent extinction — will certainly want to visit Estancia Harberton, 40 miles east of Ushuaia. If the name Harberton sounds more like the name of a village in Devon than a settlement in one of the bleakest spots of South America, you are right: the place was established in 1887 by Thomas and Mary Bridges, the first white missionaries to settle the island, who named it after Mary's birthplace in England.

Virtually every item on the estate was imported by ship from Britain, from the original wooden frame-house, which was constructed in a Devonshire carpentry shop, to a young South Devon bull, four Romney Marsh rams and a couple of Devonshire pigs. The family's amazing life among the Indians, whose languages they learnt to speak and skills they imitated, was later documented in fascinating detail by their son Lucas Bridges in *Uttermost Part of the Earth* — compulsory reading for any visitor to this area.

The book describes Thomas Bridges' painstaking compilation of a Yahgan dictionary with over 32,000 entries. Unfortunately, his business skills did not match his linguistic skills and he entrusted the finished manuscript to a glib American doctor on the Belgian Antarctic Expedition of 1898 who passed it off as his own. Luckily it eventually found its way to the British Museum where it now lies. Today the *estancia* is run by the fourth generation of the Bridges family and a visit, though expensive, is recommended. Patrick Symington provided the description below.

This is quite a popular tour with Rumbo Sur offering the trip three times a week (Sunday, Tuesday, Friday), as well as other agencies if they have enough demand of their own. However, it is expensive since it is a combined tour with a catamaran trip back from Harberton via a penguin colony and Gable Island — cost around $70 per person. The penguin colony is good, with hundreds of Megallanic Penguins and a few King Penguins. The catamaran comes close to the shore but you don't disembark.

The tour of the *estancia* itself is extremely interesting and done in a very friendly style. You see round the *estancia* buildings, including the old and current shearing sheds and gardens. On a nature trail through a pretty wood you can identify local trees and plants, and there is a reconstruction of a Yahgan hut near an actual Yaghan midden. Cake and refreshments are available (very nice!).

The only problem is that if you go on the catamaran day everybody is there at the same time — probably around 50 when we were there on a Sunday in January. There doesn't seem to be anybody who just takes you there at other times — the only option is to hire a car. It would make a nice trip with one or two nights camping, as the scenery is magnificent on the way. There are places to camp free within the *estancia* if you register at the house, and other free sites on the way. Hiring a car for the day would be about $120, but you would see the penguins!

BIBLIOGRAPHY

Below is a selection of books covering different aspects of Chile and Argentina, but the list is by no means exhaustive. Where only the British publisher is given, the book may be available in a different edition in the United States.

Guidebooks
The South American Handbook edited by Ben Box (Footprint Handbooks, Bath, England). Particularly helpful for adventurous travellers, and published annually. Each year it gets fatter and pricier.

Chile and Easter Island, a travel survival kit by Wayne Bernhardson (Lonely Planet, Australia).

Argentina, Uruguay & Paraguay, a travel survival kit by Wayne Bernhardson (Lonely Planet).

Budget Traveller's Guide to Latin America by Marjorie Cohen (Council on International Exchange, New York).

Birnbaum's South America Guide (Houghton Mifflin Co, US). Updated annually.

Tierra del Fuego by Natalie Goodall (Ediciones Shanamaüm, Buenos Aires, 1979). Bilingual text.

Guía de Excursionismo para la Cordillera de Santiago by Gaston san Roman-Herbage (Editorial Universitaria, Santiago, Chile, 1976). In Spanish.

Travelling Chile is a bimonthly bilingual magazine with lots of useful information for tourists visiting Chile. Providencia 2594, Office 321, or available from Sernatur.

Traveller's Literary Companion to South and Central America by Jason Wilson (In Print Publishing Ltd, Brighton, 1993). Includes geographical, historical, political and literary comment on each country.

Turistel, in two volumes (CTC, Santiago, updated annually). In Spanish but very detailed and up-to-date, with superb maps.

Turistel, in two volumes (CTC, Santiago, updated annually). In Spanish but very detailed and up-to-date, with superb maps.

Trekking in the Patagonian Andes by Clem Lindenmayer (Lonely Planet, 1992).

Natural history
Birds of Argentina and Uruguay by T Narosky and D Yzurieta (Vazquez Mazzini, Buenos Aires). An excellent field guide. Can be bought in BA.

The Birds of Chile, and the Adjacent Regions of Peru, Argentina and Bolivia by A W Johnson (Platt Establecimientos Gráficos, Buenos Aires, 1967). In two volumes.

Birds of the Antarctic and Sub-Antarctic by George Watson (American Geophysical Union, Washington, 1975).

South American Landbirds: a Photographic Guide to Identification by J S Dunning (Hardwood Books, Newton Square, Pennsylvania, 1981).

Paisaje de Chile, published in Chile in Spanish, English, French, available in bookshops in Santiago. Coffee table reading.

Adventure, exploration and history
Voyage of the Beagle by Charles Darwin (Cambridge University Press, 1933; paperback edition by Penguin Classics, London, 1989).

The Voyage of Charles Darwin edited by Christopher Ralling (BBC, London, 1978). A very readable selection of Darwin's autobiographical writings. Out of print but available in libraries.

In Patagonia by Bruce Chatwin (Picador, London, 1979).

The Old Patagonian Express by Paul Theroux (Penguin, London, 1979).

An Englishman in Patagonia, by John Pilkington (Century, London, 1991).

Uttermost Part of the Earth by Lucas Bridges (Hodder and Stoughton, 1947; Century Hutchinson, London, 1987).

Beyond the Silver River by Jimmy Burns (Bloomsbury, London, 1989).

Land of Tempest: Travels in Patagonia 1958-1962 by Eric Shipton (Hodder and Stoughton, London, 1963).

From the Falklands to Patagonia by Michael Mainwaring (Alison & Busby, London/New York, 1983).

Cockleshell Journey by John Ridgway (Hodder and Stoughton, 1974). Describes journey in rubber dinghy in Tierra del Fuego.

Trekking: Great Walks of the World edited by John Cleare (Unwin Hyman, London, 1988). Contains chapter on Torres del Paine.

Cucumber Sandwiches in the Andes by John Ure (Constable, London, 1973). Describes a crossing on horseback between Chile and Argentina.

Tschiffely's Ride by A F Tschiffely (Heinemann, London, 1934). Describes 10,000 mile ride from Argentina to Washington. A classic.

Up, Into the Singing Mountain by Richard Llewellyn (New English Library, 1985). Hero of *How Green Was My Valley* seeks adventure among the Welsh settlers in Patagonia.

Far Away and Long Ago by W H Hudson (Eland/Hippocrene 1987). Reprint of a classic account, written in 1918, of a naturalist's childhood in Argentina.

Back to Cape Horn by Rosie Swale (Fontana, London, 1986). A journey on horseback down the length of Chile.

Historia del Andinismo en Chile by Gaston San Ramón Herbage (published in Santiago, Chile, 1989). Includes some interesting maps (with routes) of the Chilean *cordillera*. In Spanish.

Adventura is a monthly magazine published by the Sociedad Chilena de Exploracíon, Londres 67, Santiago. In Spanish.

Alfonsin by Jimmy Burns (Bloomsbury, 1987).

A House Divided: Argentina 1880-1980 by Eduardo Crawley (C Hurst and Co, 1984).

A State of Fear by Andrew Graham-Yooll (Eland/Hippocrene Books, 1986). The years of the 'disappearances' by the editor of the Buenos Aires Herald.

Chile: Death in the South by Jacobo Timerman (Picador, 1987).

Health guides

Travellers' Health: How to Stay Healthy Abroad edited by Dr Richard Dawood (Oxford University Press, 1994).

OTHER BRADT GUIDES TO SOUTH AMERICA

Backpacking and Trekking in Peru and Bolivia by Hilary Bradt.
Sixth edition (1995) The classic guide for walkers and nature lovers.

Backcountry Brazil by Alex Bradbury.
Three areas are covered in depth: Amazonia, the Pantanal, and the
north-east coast.

Venezuela by Hilary Dunsterville Branch.
A guide for eco-tourists emphasising the mountains, jungles and
national parks with several sections specifically on hiking.

Climbing and Hiking in Ecuador by Rob Rachowiecki & Betsy
Wagenhauser.
The definitive guide to the volcanoes, mountains and cloudforests of
Ecuador, by two former residents.

South American Ski Guide by Chris Lizza.
Details of 35 ski centres mostly in Chile and Argentina, with ski
history and trail maps.

This is just a selection of our books for adventurous travellers. Send
for our latest catalogue.

Bradt Publications, 41 Nortoft Rd, Chalfont St Peter, Bucks
SL9 0LA, England. Tel/fax: 01494 873478

Bradt Publications

Travel Guides

41 Nortoft Road • Chalfont St Peter • Bucks • SL9 0LA • England Fax/Telephone: 01494 873478

December 1996

Dear readers,

This book is a group effort. You are part of the group and your efforts will help make the next edition, due in 1998, as up to date as is possible to be in the changing conditions of Chile and Argentina.

Do write to me. Each person's journey is unique, each traveller has his/her own insights and experiences. Everyone has something to contribute – a new camp site, a clearer description of an overgrown trail, a needed change on a map, or – best of all – an entirely new hike discovered by looking beyond the guidebooks to the adventures offered by two countries of infinite possibilities.

And remember: as a backpacker you are never lost, you are seeing new places!

With best wishes,

Hilary Bradt

Hilary Bradt

INDEX